The Competency Crisis

The Competency Crisis

Will Stickle

Contents

1

Introduction

Ayn Rand's Atlas Shrugged stands as one of the most prescient works of the 20th century, a dystopian novel that has transcended fiction to become a mirror reflecting the grim realities of the contemporary Western world. Published in 1957, Atlas Shrugged explores the consequences of a society that abandons individual responsibility, meritocracy, and the entrepreneurism—values that have been the bedrock of Western civilization. In Rand's narrative, later adopted by Mike Judge for "Idiocracy", the world's most productive citizens, the "men of the mind," go on strike, retreating from a society that punishes their success and rewards mediocrity. The resulting chaos, marked by economic collapse, political corruption, and social decay, serves as a stark warning of what happens when a civilization forsakes the very principles that drive progress. Collapse, corruption, and decay all to evident in all dectors of our modern society.

Today, we find ourselves living in a world that increasingly resembles the dystopian society Rand envisioned. The Western nations, once the paragons of innovation, freedom, and prosperity, are now in the throes of a deepening competency crisis. This crisis, characterized by the decline of meritocratic values, the erosion of individual responsibility, and the rise of entitlement, is undermining the very foundation of Western civilization. What Rand depicted as a fictional scenario in Atlas

Shrugged has become a haunting reality—a reality where the competent are shackled and vastly outnumbered by the incompetent, where producers are exploited by looters, and where the once-great engines of industry and progress are grinding to a halt.

The Collapse of Meritocracy and the Rise of Mediocrity

At the core of Rand's warning is the collapse of the meritocracy, the system in which individuals rise or fall based on their abilities coupled with effort and achievement. In Atlas Shrugged, a world is presented in which merit is no longer the currency of success. Instead, political connections, bureaucratic maneuvering or social favouritism determine outcomes. The innovators, the builders, the creators—those who contribute most to society—are marginalized and oppressed by a system that prioritizes mediocrity and punishes excellence.

This dystopian vision is not just a cautionary tale but a reflection of the current state of the West. Today, the meritocratic values that once propelled the West to unparalleled heights of achievement have been systematically dismantled for decades. Affirmative action policies, diversity quotas (DEI), and the glorification of victimhood have created a culture where merit is secondary to identity and group affiliation. The result is a society where average (or less) is not only tolerated but celebrated, where the pursuit of excellence is seen as a threat rather than a virtue.

This erosion is evident in every sector, from academia to industry to government. In education, standards are lowered to ensure equal outcomes rather than equal opportunities, leading to a generation of graduates who are ill-prepared for the challenges of the real world. In the corporate world, businesses prioritize social justice over profitability, hiring based on identity rather than competence. In politics, leaders are chosen for their ability to appease, at best, rather than their ability to lead, resulting in a governance that is reactive, short-sighted, and ultimately destructive. Oh, and extrememly corrupt.

The Abandonment of Individual Responsibility

Another central theme of Atlas Shrugged is the abandonment of individual responsibility. Rand champions the idea that individuals are responsible for their own lives, that success and failure are the results of one's own choices and actions. The society depicted is one in which this principle has been turned on its head. Responsibility is collectivized, and individuals are absolved of the consequences of their actions. The state steps in to redistribute wealth, resources, and opportunities, ostensibly in the name of fairness, but in reality, to the detriment of all.

In the modern West, we see this abandonment of individual responsibility manifesting in various ways. The welfare state has grown to a point where dependency is the norm, and personal accountability is the exception. Government programs designed to provide a safety net have become permanent crutches, discouraging self-reliance and fostering a culture of entitlement. The result is a populace that looks to the state for solutions to every problem, from economic woes to personal failings, rather than taking ownership of their lives.

This cultural shift is particularly evident in the younger generations, who have been raised in a world where the idea of working for success is increasingly replaced by the expectation that success should be handed to them. The rise of "safe spaces" in universities, the decline in trade work, and the glorification of social justice over individual achievement are all symptoms of a society that has forgotten the value of personal responsibility.

Envy, Entitlement, and the Decline of the West

Rand also explores the corrosive effects of envy and entitlement, which she saw as the primary drivers of societal decay. In Atlas Shrugged, these forces lead to the vilification of the successful and the elevation of the mediocre. The competent are burdened with supporting the incompetent, not through their own choice, but through the coercive power of the state. This looter mentality, as Rand described it, is a parasitic relationship that ultimately leads to the destruction of both the looters and the producers.

In the contemporary West, envy and entitlement have become pervasive. The success of others is often seen as a threat, and there is a growing belief that wealth and power should be redistributed, not earned. This mentality has permeated every level of society, from the political rhetoric of wealth redistribution to the social movements that demand equality of outcome rather than equality of opportunity. The result is a culture where ambition is stifled, innovation is discouraged, and the drive to excel is replaced by the desire to conform.

The parallels between the world of Atlas Shrugged and our current reality are striking. Rand's dystopia was a world where the competent few were sacrificed on the altar of the incompetent many, where individual achievement was punished, and where the pursuit of excellence is replaced by the demand for conformity. A world we are dangerously close to realizing. Rand's warning was not just a description of a potential future—it was a call to action. The crisis facing the West is not inevitable. It is the result of choices, and it can be reversed by making different choices. To avoid this fate we must reclaim our values, we must reject the looter mentality and reassert the primacy of the producer. It is the only way to hope to restore ourselves to our rightful place and prevent the dystopian vision of Atlas Shrugged, or worse, Idiocracy, from becoming our reality.

This is the context in which we must view the current state of the West—The Western world stands at a perilous crossroads. The foundations that once made us a beacon of progress and prosperity are crumbling under the weight of a deepening competency crisis, a precipitous decline in fertility rates, and the erosion of the values that have historically defined and sustained our societies. This book is a call to action—an urgent plea to recognize the dangers that lie ahead and to chart a course that will restore the principles of individual responsibility, meritocracy, and the entrepreneurial spirit before it is too late.

The Competency Crisis: A Civilization in Decline

At the heart of the West's current predicament is a competency crisis—a pervasive decline in the standards of excellence, innovation, and leadership that once drove our societies forward. This crisis is not merely a consequence of poor governance or economic mismanagement; it is a symptom of a much deeper cultural decay. We have allowed mediocrity to replace merit, and in doing so, we have created a society where the most capable are shackled by the least competent.

This book aims to shine a light on the causes and consequences of this crisis, to explore how a culture of complacency, entitlement, and envy has undermined the values of hard work, individual responsibility, and excellence that once defined the Western world. It will delve into the systemic issues—ranging from the degradation of the education system to the rise of bureaucratic bloat—that have facilitated this decline, and it will offer suggestions for reversing this course.

The Decline in Fertility: A Symptom of Cultural Decay

The dramatic decline in fertility rates across Western nations is not just a demographic challenge; it is a sign of a civilization that has lost confidence in its future. Fertility rates are falling because people no longer believe in the promise of tomorrow, because the values that once encouraged the growth and perpetuation of our societies have been eroded by nihilism, materialism, and a retreat from the responsibilities of family and community.

This book will explore the cultural and societal factors that have contributed to this decline, examining how the loss of faith in the future, coupled with the rise of individualism unmoored from responsibility, has led to a world where fewer people see the value in bringing new life into the world. It will argue that reversing this trend requires a fundamental shift in how we view the role of the family, the importance of community, and the responsibilities we owe to future generations.

Underlying both the competency crisis and the decline in fertility is a broader erosion of the values that have historically sustained civilization. The very values that drove the West's success—are being dismantled by a culture that prioritizes equality of outcome over equality of opportunity, that punishes excellence, and elevates entitlement over effort.

This book will argue that the West's current decline is not inevitable but is the result of a deliberate abandonment of these values. It will explore how envy, entitlement, and a misguided sense of justice have undermined the work ethic, stifled innovation, and created a society where the pursuit of excellence is seen as a threat rather than a virtue. By reclaiming these values, we can not only halt the decline but reverse it, restoring the West to its rightful place as a leader in the world. We will not only diagnose the problems facing the West but to offer a blueprint for renewal, outlining possible paths forward. It will argue that the only way to reverse the competency crisis is to reassert the importance of merit and excellence in all aspects of society, from education to industry to government. It will propose solutions to the fertility crisis that go beyond mere economic incentives, focusing instead on the cultural renewal that is necessary to create a place where people want to build families and invest in the future.

The urgency of this mission cannot be overstated. The choices we make today will determine whether the West continues its descent into mediocrity and decay, or whether it rises once again to reclaim its place as the driving force of human progress. This book is a call to arms for those who believe that the future of Western civilization is worth fighting for—and that the time to fight is now. The Western world is (probably) not collapsing because of external forces or hostile adversaries; it is crumbling from within, a victim of its own internal failures. The decline we witness today is the direct consequence of a systematic abandonment of the values that once made us the epicentre of progress, innovation, and prosperity. A decline that can be reversed with the renewed appreciation for individual responsibility, merit, and entrepreneurialism.

Individual Responsibility: At the heart of the West's success has always been the principle that individuals are accountable for their own lives. This ethos of self-reliance and personal accountability has driven our greatest achievements, fostering a culture where success is earned, and failure is an opportunity for growth. However, over the past several decades, this value has been steadily eroded. The rise of the welfare state, the increasing dependency on government support, and the cultural shift towards victimhood and entitlement have created a society where individuals are no longer encouraged to take responsibility for their own lives. Instead, they are taught to look to the state for solutions, to blame external factors for their failures, and to expect rewards without effort.

Meritocracy: The decline of meritocracy is perhaps the most visible sign of the our internal decay. Meritocracy, the idea that people should rise based on their abilities and efforts, has been the cornerstone of Western progress. It has driven innovation, economic growth, and social mobility. But today, meritocracy is under assault. The obsession with equality of outcome, rather than equality of opportunity, has led to a culture where excellence is punished, and mediocrity is rewarded. Affirmative action, DEI, and the prioritization of identity over competence have created a system where merit is no longer the primary determinant of success. This has resulted in a decline in standards across all sectors of society, from education to business to government, and has stifled the very innovation that we were once known for.

Entrepreneurialism: The entrepreneurial spirit—the drive to create, innovate, and take risks—has always been a defining characteristic of the West. It is this spirit that fuelled the industrial revolution, drove technological advancements, and created the prosperity that we have enjoyed for centuries. But this spirit is now under threat. Overregulation, punitive taxation, and a culture that increasingly views profit as immoral have stifled entrepreneurship. The result is a stagnating economy, declining innovation, and a generation of young people who are more interested in secure, risk-free careers than in the challenges and rewards of entrepreneurship.

This thesis contends that our decline is not the result of external pressures but of a deliberate and systematic abandonment of these core values. The internal rot that has taken hold of Western civilization—manifested in the competency crisis, the decline in fertility, and the erosion of societal values—is self-inflicted. To reverse this decline, the West must reclaim these foundational principles. It must reassert the importance of individual responsibility, it must restore meritocracy, and it must reignite the entrepreneurial spirit.

Only by doing so can the West hope to arrest its decay and restore the vitality that once made it the leader of the free world.

2

The Fall of the Producer

C elebrating the Unexceptional

In the West today, the ordinary (or worse) has gained a troubling foothold, pushing aside excellence and competence in nearly every aspect of life. This transformation isn't accidental; it mirrors the cultural and institutional devolution that has systematically devalued merit, punished ambition, and elevated the mundane over the exceptional. This shift is a clear symptom of the broader decline in our civilization, showing a society that has lost its drive for success and its respect for those who fuel progress.

At its core, this shift is a cultural realignment that has warped what our society values. Where Western culture once celebrated innovators, creators, and trailblazers, those who expanded the boundaries of possibility and set new standards for excellence, it now instead elevates the unremarkable, the perverse, and at times, the obscene. The pursuit of greatness finds itself increasingly met with suspicion, resentment, or outright hostility.

Success, which was once deemed as the the positive outcome of hard work, talent, and perseverance, is now frequently dismissed as a product of privilege, luck, and exploitation of the masses. When society scorns over achievers, what drives individuals to strive for it? While that same society basks in the comforts brought forth by over achievers of times gone by.

The entertainment industry, social media, and education systems all mirror this strange cultural shift. Reality television frequently glorifies the lowest common denominator, social media platforms prioritize the unremarkable over the exceptional, and schools often focus more on inclusivity and conformity rather than critical thinking and intellectual rigour. The message is clear: the average isn't just acceptable; it's desirable. Everybody gets a ribbon

Institutionalizing the Unexceptional

This embrace of the weird and the weak has not only taken root culturally but is also being institutionalized across various sectors. In education, the drive for excellence has been replaced by grade inflation, grade curves and lowered standards to protect students' self-esteem and competition is often vilified. This approach leaves a generation unprepared for the real world's challenges, where competence is crucial and excellence is rightly rewarded.

In the workplace, merit-based promotions are increasingly overshadowed by considerations of Diversity, Equity, and Inclusion (DEI). While these goals could be argued commendable in theory, they often lead to the elevation of individuals based on factors other than competence or contribution, creating a workforce where the status quo is maintained, and excellence is sidelined or even punished.

Government policies also contribute to this trend. Regulations intended to create fairness often stifle the necessary competition that drives down prices and promotes excellence. Tax systems that disproportionately penalize the successful discourage innovation and entrepreneurship, while welfare programs, though arguably necessary, can sometimes create situations where staying within the system seems more beneficial than striving for improvement through hard work.

The embrace of the average has far-reaching and damaging consequences. Economically, it leads to stagnation. When accomplishment is no longer rewarded, there is little incentive to innovate or strive for greatness, slowing progress. The West, once the global leader in technological and industrial innovation, now risks falling behind emerging economies that still value and reward achievement.

Socially, rewarding mediocrity breeds resentment and division. Those who strive for excellence become disillusioned, withdrawing from a society that no longer values their contributions. This withdrawal creates a vacuum, filled by those less competent but more compliant, a scenario vividly depicted in Ayn Rand's Atlas Shrugged.

Moreover, a culture that doesn't value achievement erodes the moral fabric of society. It becomes comfortable with the lowest standards, accepts dishonesty and laziness as normal, and ultimately loses its sense of purpose and direction.

Reversing the Tide

To reverse course, a radical cultural and institutional shift is needed. We must return to the values that once made us great: a celebration of excellence, a commitment to meritocracy, and a belief in individual responsibility. This means holding people to higher standards, rewarding achievement, and fostering a culture that encourages striving for greatness.

Educational systems must be reformed to emphasize knowledge over inclusion. The workplace should focus on rewarding those who contribute the most, not just those who meet diversity criteria. Government policies and contracts should encourage competition and innovation, not stifle them in the name of equality and blatant corruption.

Most importantly, this shift must start with the individual. Each person must reject settling for less than the best, despite obstacles. Only by reclaiming the values of excellence and competence can the West hope to halt its decline and regain its position as a global leader.

This isn't an inevitable consequence of modernity; it's a choice—a choice that can be reversed. Consider this a call to action for those who refuse to accept the average as the norm, who believe that we can once again become a society that celebrates greatness and rewards competence. The future of Western civilization depends on it.

Erosion of Leadership

Leadership, once the cornerstone of progress and stability, has undergone a profound transformation over the past few decades. Where leaders were once chosen for their merit, vision, and ability to deliver results, today's political and corporate leadership increasingly reflects a shift toward compromise-driven decision-making at best, and outright corruption at worst. This shift is not just a change in style but a fundamental departure from the principles that once ensured western preeminence. The consequences are widespread incompetence, stagnation, and the loss of public trust in institutions.

Traditionally, leadership in both political and corporate spheres was built on expertise and experience. Leaders were those who demonstrated exceptional abilities, a clear vision for the future, and the capacity to execute that vision effectively. Political leaders were expected to guide their nations through complex challenges, making decisions based on said expertise and experience, and include ethical considerations. Corporate leaders, similarly, were chosen for their ability to innovate, drive profitability, and steer their companies through competitive markets.

In this framework, leadership was synonymous with responsibility, accountability, and excellence. Leaders were held to the highest standards, their success measured by tangible outcomes like economic growth, social stability, and technological innovation. This approach was instrumental in the West's rise to global dominance, fostering an environment where the best and brightest could ascend to positions of power, driving progress and prosperity.

Noticing the Shift

In recent decades there has been a noticeable shift in our traditional approach to leadership. This shift has been driven by several factors, including the rise of identity politics, the influence of special interest groups, and the growing emphasis on short-term gains over long-term vision.

In politics, this shift is most evident in how leaders are chosen and how they govern. Electoral success often hinges on a candidate's ability to cater to the most vocal segments of the electorate, rather than on their ability to address the complex issues facing their nation. Politicians increasingly pander to populist sentiments, promising quick fixes and immediate rewards while avoiding the tough decisions true leadership requires. The result is a political landscape dominated by leaders more concerned with maintaining popularity than with implementing effective policies.

Corporate leadership has not been immune to this trend. In many companies, the criteria for leadership have shifted from a focus on business acumen and strategic thinking to an emphasis on appearance of social responsibility, diversity initiatives, and media/public relations.

Moreover, the erosion of leadership has had a cascading effect on the workforce. Employees who see their leaders prioritizing compromise over excellence are less likely to be motivated to perform at their best. The devaluation of calibre at the top trickles down through the ranks, leading to a general decline in organizational competence, morale, and ultimately productiveness.

Restoring True Leadership

Reversing the damage caused requires a return to the principles of ability and accountability. Political and corporate leaders must once again be chosen for their abilities, vision, and commitment to delivering tangible results rather than for their skill in navigating the politics of compromise.

In the political arena, this means embracing leaders willing to make tough decisions, even when those decisions are unpopular. It means valuing long-term vision over short-term gains and requires a public willing to support leaders who prioritize the nation's future over immediate gratification. Voters must demand more from their leaders—more competence, more integrity, and more courage—and reward those who demonstrate these qualities.

In the corporate world, the focus must shift back to innovation, profitability, and creating value. Boards of directors and shareholders must hold executives accountable for their performance, prioritizing competence and strategic thinking over the ability to appease external pressures. Companies that prioritize this in their leadership will not only outperform their competitors but also set a standard that others will be forced to follow.

Ultimately, restoring true leadership in the West requires a cultural shift. The erosion of leadership is both a symptom and a cause of the broader decay of Western civilization. It reflects a society that has lost sight of the principles that made it great and perpetuates the very problems it was meant to solve. By understanding how and why this shift occurred, and by committing to reversing it, we can begin the process of restoration.

Impact on Innovation

Innovation has long been the engine driving Western civilization's remarkable progress, from the Industrial Revolution to the digital age. It powers economic growth, enhances quality of life, and secures a nation's position on the global stage. However, the current competency crisis threatens to extinguish this essential spark. As bureaucratic inertia overtakes visionary leadership, we face the grim prospect of technological and industrial stagnation. This stagnation not only hampers economic progress but also leaves us increasingly vulnerable in a world where other nations are rapidly advancing.

This decline in innovation is evident across multiple sectors. In academia, research that pushes the boundaries of knowledge is increasingly sidelined in favour of studies that align with prevailing social or political agendas. In industry, the focus on short-term profits and avoiding controversy has led to a reduction in investment in research and development (R&D), the very lifeblood of technological advancement. Companies that once prided themselves on their ability to innovate are now more concerned with managing public relations crises or virtue signalling than with developing the next groundbreaking technology.

The tech industry, once the crown jewel of Western innovation, now starkly exemplifies this trend. While once the undisputed leader in technological development, it now struggles to maintain its competitive edge. The focus on diversity quotas, social justice initiatives, and the appeasement of activist shareholders has diverted attention away from core technological challenges. As a result, many tech companies are losing ground to more focused and merit-driven competitors in Asia and elsewhere.

"Bureaucratic Inertia"

Bureaucratic inertia is a significant factor contributing to the stagnation. In both government and industry, layers of regulation, red tape, and risk aversion have created an environment where new ideas struggle to gain traction. This inertia is particularly damaging in industries that require substantial investment and long development cycles, such as energy, manufacturing, and aerospace.

In the past, Western governments and corporations were willing to take bold risks in pursuit of technological breakthroughs. The space race, the development of the internet, and the rapid industrialization of the post-war era were all driven by a willingness to venture into the unknown, to push beyond the limits of what was considered possible. Today, however, that spirit of adventure has been replaced by a culture of caution. Regulatory frameworks designed to ensure safety and fairness have become obstacles to progress, stifling the very innovation they were meant to protect.

This bureaucratic inertia is particularly evident in the energy sector. The energy infrastructure, once a model of innovation and efficiency, is now aging and increasingly reliant on outdated technologies. Efforts to modernize this infrastructure are often hampered by regulatory delays and legal challenges. Meanwhile, other nations, unburdened by such constraints, are rapidly advancing in areas such as nuclear energy, renewable technologies, and energy storage. The failure to innovate in this critical sector not only threatens its economic future but also its national security, as energy independence becomes increasingly difficult to maintain.

Economic Consequences

In the manufacturing sector, this decline has led to a loss of competitiveness. Once-dominant industries are being outpaced by more agile and innovative competitors in Asia, where investment in automation, robotics, and advanced manufacturing techniques is driving rapid industrial growth. The result is a hollowing out of the Western industrial base, with factories closing, jobs being lost, and communities falling into economic despair and addiction.

In the technology sector, it has led to a concentration of power in a few dominant companies, buying up anything resembling competition, reducing the incentive to innovate. This concentration has also led to monopolistic practices, where companies are more focused on maintaining market dominance and big government approval than on developing new technologies or market forces. The result is a tech landscape where incremental improvements are celebrated as major breakthroughs, and where truly disruptive innovation is increasingly rare.

Furthermore, the failure to innovate has significant implications for global competitiveness. As other nations invest heavily in R&D and cultivate a culture of excellence, the West risks falling behind in critical areas such as artificial intelligence, biotechnology, and space exploration. This decline not only threatens economic prosperity but also geopolitical stability, as technological superiority is a key component of national power in the modern world.

The Vulnerability of the West in a Rapidly Changing World

This vulnerability is compounded by the fact that other nations are not standing still. China, for example, has made innovation a cornerstone of its national strategy, investing heavily in areas such as artificial intelligence, quantum computing, and space exploration. Similarly, countries like South Korea, Japan, and Israel have built their economies on a foundation of continuous innovation, challenging the West's dominance in key industries.

The West's failure to address its competency crisis leaves it increasingly dependent on the technological advancements of others. This dependency is not just an economic issue; it is a strategic vulnerability that can be exploited by rival nations. As the West continues to lose its technological edge, it risks losing its ability to shape the global order, defend its interests, and secure its future.

Reigniting Innovation

Reversing this trend requires a fundamental shift in how the West approaches leadership, education, and economic policy. We must return to a culture that values merit, rewards excellence, and encourages risk-taking. This means dismantling the bureaucratic obstacles, reforming education systems to prioritize critical thinking and problem-solving, and creating an economic environment that incentivizes investment in R&D.

Education is another critical area for reform. To foster innovation, the West must prioritize STEM (science, technology, engineering, and mathematics) education It also means fostering a culture of intellectual curiosity, where questioning the status quo and challenging existing paradigms are encouraged rather than discouraged.

Finally, economic policy must be aligned. This means reducing regulatory barriers, providing incentives for investment in R&D, and creating a business environment that rewards risk-taking and long-term thinking. It also means addressing the issue of income inequality, not by redistributing wealth, but by creating opportunities for all individuals to succeed based on their abilities and contributions.

3

The Fertility Decline

Demographic Suicide

The term "demographic suicide" might sound alarmist, but it accurately captures the self-inflicted crisis facing Western nations today. Birth rates across the West have plummeted to levels that are unsustainable for the long-term viability of these societies. A civilization that fails to replace its population is one that is on a path to extinction, and the West is dancing perilously close to that threshold. Unlike the natural ebb and flow of population dynamics observed throughout history, this demographic decline is driven by a series of deliberate choices that reflect a broader loss of confidence in the future. Understanding the reasons behind this decline is crucial if we are to reverse course and avoid the unpleasant consequences of demographic suicide.

One of the primary drivers of falling birth rates is a cultural shift away from traditional family values toward a more selfish and materialistic worldview. In the past, having a family and raising children were once seen as playing central role in a fulfilling life. Societal norms encouraged marriage and childbearing as essential components of personal identity and social stability.

However, over the past several decades, these values have been increasingly replaced by a focus on personal freedom and consumerism. The idea of self-fulfillment has become intertwined with material success, with much less emphasis on family life. This shift is reflected in the delayed age of marriage, the postponement of childbearing, and the decision by many to remain childless altogether. The pursuit of personal goals and lifestyles, often at the expense of starting a family, has become the norm.

This trend is particularly pronounced among women, who have made significant strides in education and the workforce. While the empowerment of women is undoubtedly a positive development, it has also contributed to the declining birth rate as more women choose to prioritize their careers over having children. The societal expectation that women should be able to "have it all"—a successful career, personal freedom, and a family—often leads to a delay in childbearing until it is biologically more challenging or even impossible.

Misplaced Feminism

Another contributing factor, is the influence of what can be described as misplaced feminism. While the feminist movement has seemingly achieved some progress in securing equal rights and opportunities for women, certain ideological offshoots have inadvertently contributed to the current crisis. By promoting a narrative that equates motherhood with oppression and traditional family structures with patriarchy, , feminism has discouraged many women from embracing the role of motherhood. The elevation of career over family as the primary measure of a woman's success has led to the devaluation of childbearing and rearing as fulfilling and important aspects of life. Rather than empowering women to make balanced life choices, this version of feminism has created an environment where the decision to start a family is often seen as a betrayal of personal ambition, leading to long-term demographic consequences.

Economic factors also play a significant role in the decline of birth rates. The cost of raising children has skyrocketed, making family life increasingly unaffordable for many. Housing prices in major cities have soared, education costs have ballooned, and the overall expense of providing a decent standard of living has become prohibitive for young couples. These financial pressures are compounded by the fact that wages have stagnated, and job security has diminished, particularly for younger generations.

The result is that many young people feel economically unprepared to start a family. The prospect of raising children in an environment where financial stability is uncertain can be daunting. This economic anxiety is exacerbated by the lack of supportive family policies in many Western nations. While some countries offer generous parental leave and childcare subsidies, others provide minimal support, making it difficult for parents to balance work and family life. Moreover, the cultural glorification of consumerism and the expectation of maintaining a certain lifestyle also discourage family formation.

The Decline of Religion and the Loss of Purpose

Another significant contributing factor is the decline of religious faith and the corresponding loss of a sense of higher purpose. Historically, religion played a central role in encouraging family formation and childbearing. Most major religions promote the idea that having children is a moral duty and a way to contribute to the continuation of the community and faith.

In the secularized West, however, religious adherence has waned dramatically. The decline in religious belief has been accompanied by a broader existential crisis, where individuals struggle to find meaning and purpose in their lives. In the absence of religious or spiritual motivations, the incentive to have children diminishes. For many, the decision to is no longer seen as part of a larger moral or communal obligation but rather as a personal choice, one that can be easily dismissed.

Government policies—or the lack thereof—also play a crucial role. Many Western nations have failed to implement tax policies that support family formation and child-rearing. While some countries, like those in Scandinavia, have introduced generous family benefits, others have been slow to adopt such measures. In some cases, government policies have inadvertently discouraged childbearing. High taxation, stringent labor laws, and restrictive housing regulations make it difficult for young people to achieve the financial stability necessary for starting a family. In other instances, the welfare state and family court systems have created disincentives for family formation by providing sufficient support for individuals to live independently without the need for a family network.

The Consequences

The consequences of falling birth rates are potentially catastrophic. Economically, a shrinking population leads to a reduced labor force, which in turn slows economic growth. Fewer workers mean fewer consumers, which can lead to a deflationary spiral where demand for goods and services declines, leading to lower economic output and reduced investment. This economic stagnation can be particularly severe in countries where the population is aging rapidly, as the burden of supporting an increasingly elderly population falls on a shrinking base of younger workers.

Socially, it can lead to the erosion of communities and the weakening of social bonds. As populations shrink, especially in rural areas, communities can become depopulated, leading to the closure of schools, businesses, and other essential services. This depopulation can create a sense of isolation and despair among those who remain, further accelerating the decline.

Culturally, we are threatening the very survival of Western civilization. A civilization that does not reproduce itself is one that will eventually disappear, replaced by those that do. This demographic suicide is not just a numbers game; it is a profound existential crisis. The values, traditions, and achievements of the western world are at risk of being lost if there are not enough people to carry them forward.

Reversing the trend of demographic decline require decisive, multi-faceted actions at both the governmental and societal levels. This is not merely about addressing the symptoms but tackling the root causes that have led us to this precarious situation. Governments must take the lead in implementing policies that make family formation more attainable. This includes creating affordable housing initiatives and offering substantial tax incentives for families. By doing so, the state can create an environment where starting and raising a family is not only feasible but also encouraged.

At the same time, there must be a realignment that redefines personal fulfillment to include family life as a core component. This means challenging the dominant narrative that suggests career success and personal freedom are inherently at odds with raising children. Media, educational institutions, and community leaders must promote the idea that having children is both a personal and societal good—an essential contribution to the continuity and vitality of our civilization.

Politically, leaders must prioritize this issue, recognizing demographic decline as a critical threat to national survival. This may require difficult decisions, such as rethinking immigration policies to prioritize family-friendly outcomes and investing in infrastructure that supports young families. The urgency of this crisis cannot be overstated; the actions we take today will determine whether the West can sustain itself in the long run.

Nihilism

The crisis we are facing is an existential one, one that is contributing significantly to the dramatic decline in fertility rates across the region. This crisis is rooted in a pervasive sense of nihilism—a belief that life is inherently meaningless and that the future holds little promise. As faith in the future diminishes, so too does the motivation to bring new life into the world. Compounding this issue is a widespread retreat from the values of self-reliance and individual responsibility, the foundations upon which strong, stable families are built. Together, these forces are driving a demographic collapse that threatens the long-term survival of the West.

Nihilism is the belief that life lacks inherent meaning. This has become increasingly prevalent in Western culture. This philosophical outlook, once confined to the fringes of intellectual discourse, has now permeated mainstream society, influencing everything from art and literature to politics and personal attitudes. The rise of nihilism can be traced to several sources, including the decline of religious belief and the growing perception that the future is bleak.

The decline of religious belief is a central factor. For centuries, religion provided a framework for understanding the world and one's place within it. It offered a sense of purpose and a vision of the future that extended beyond the individual's life. As religious adherence has waned, many people have found themselves without a coherent worldview or a sense of higher purpose. This spiritual void has been filled by nihilistic attitudes, where the absence of meaning leads to apathy, despair, and a lack of motivation to contribute to the future.

Adding to this is the legacy of catastrophic predictions from influential works like "The Population Bomb" by Paul Ehrlich and the Club of Rome's "Limits to Growth." These works, despite being thoroughly debunked, instilled a deep-seated fear of overpopulation and resource scarcity in the collective consciousness of the West. The idea that the world is on an inevitable path to destruction due to unchecked population growth has led to a pervasive sense of hopelessness and a reluctance to have children. The narrative that bringing new life into the world is irresponsible has taken root, further feeding the nihilistic outlook that has gripped many. The abandonment of traditional social structures—such as the family and community, has further fuelled the rise of nihilism. As these structures have been devalued, individuals have become increasingly isolated, disconnected from the broader social fabric that once gave life meaning and direction. The breakdown of these bonds has left many people feeling adrift, with little sense of responsibility to themselves, never mind others or future generations.

"The future is bleak" has exacerbated the spread. Economic uncertainty, political instability, environmental concerns, and the rapid pace of technological change have all contributed to a widespread sense of pessimism about the future. When people believe that the world is on a downward trajectory, they are less likely to feel that bringing children into such a world is a responsible or desirable choice.

One of the most direct ways this manifests is in the growing number of people who choose to remain childless, either by delaying or altogether rejecting the idea of having children. For some, this decision is driven by a sense of existential dread—why bring a child into a world that seems doomed? For others, the decision is rooted in a broader sense of apathy or a focus on self-gratification, where the responsibilities of parenthood are seen as burdensome and incompatible with a lifestyle centred on personal freedom and pleasure.

This decline in fertility is not just a matter of individual choice; it reflects a broader cultural shift away from the idea that raising children is a vital and fulfilling part of life. In a society increasingly dominated by bad attitudes, the nuclear family—once the cornerstone of social stability and the vehicle for transmitting values and culture to the next generation—has been de-emphasized or even vilified

Retreat from Self-Reliance

Closely related is the retreat from self-reliance, a value that has historically been central to the Western ethos. Self-reliance is the belief that individuals are responsible for their own lives, that they must work hard, make sacrifices, and rely on their own abilities to achieve their goals. This value has been a driving force behind the success of our civilization, encouraging a culture of innovation, entrepreneurship, and resilience.

In recent decades, this has been steadily eroded, replaced by a growing dependency on the state and a epidemic of entitlement. This shift has profound implications for fertility rates, as the retreat undermines the very foundations of family life.

Raising a family requires a significant investment of time, energy, and resources. It demands a level of commitment and resilience that is incompatible with the mentality of dependency that has taken root in much of the West. When individuals are conditioned to expect that their needs will be met by the state, or that they are entitled to a certain standard of living without having to work for it, they are less likely to develop the qualities of self-discipline and responsibility that are necessary for successful parenthood.

The retreat from self-reliance is closely tied to the decline of long-term thinking. When we are focused solely on immediate gratification, we are less likely to plan for the future or to make the sacrifices necessary for it. This short-term mindset, which is reinforced by consumer culture and the welfare state, contributes to the decision by many to delay or even forgo childbearing altogether.

As more people become dependent on the state, the social safety net becomes strained, leading to economic instability and increased taxation. This, in turn, creates an environment where starting a family becomes even more difficult, as the financial burdens of parenthood increase. The result is a vicious cycle where declining self-reliance leads to declining fertility, which in turn intensifies the economic and social challenges.

Religious and spiritual communities have a crucial role to play in this renewal, offering a sense of purpose and belonging that transcends material success. Educational institutions, too, must be at the forefront of this change, instilling in young people the importance of life, family, and community as foundational elements of a meaningful existence. Additionally, there must be a revival of the value of self—a renewed emphasis on personal responsibility, hard work, and planning for the future. This includes reforming welfare systems to reduce dependency and incentivize work and family formation, fostering a culture of self-reliance where raising a family is seen as a worthwhile and achievable goal.

The broader shift toward long-term thinking is essential. The decisions we make today will echo through generations, determining whether our society thrives or declines. By fostering a culture where family is once again seen as the foundation of society, we can ensure that the West has a future worth looking forward to.

The decline in birth rates and the resulting shrinking population across Western nations are not merely demographic phenomena—they are harbingers of seismic shifts with far-reaching significance. A civilization that fails to sustain its population is one that slowly erodes its foundations, risking not just economic and political instability but also the loss of its cultural identity and continuity. The long-term sustainability of the West is under threat, as the societal impacts of fewer children ripple through every facet of life, undermining the structures and values that have historically defined us.

One of the most immediate implications of birth rates is continuity. Culture is not a static entity; it is a living, evolving expression of a society's values, traditions, and collective memory. It is transmitted from one generation to the next through families, educational institutions, and social practices. As the number of children decreases, so too does the ability of a society to pass on its cultural heritage.

In many Western countries, this problem is already evident. Languages, traditions, and customs that have been handed down for generations are slowly fading as the populations that sustain them shrink. This loss is particularly acute in rural areas and among minority communities, where it can lead to the disappearance of entire ways of life. As these elements vanish, the rich tapestry of our hand crafted world becomes increasingly threadbare, reducing the diversity and vibrancy that once characterized it.

Of course this weakening has broader implications for national identity. We must at least on some level agree about who we are and where we're going to maintain social cohesion. It provides a common framework within which one can understand their place in the world and their relationship to others. As birth rates plummet and cultural continuity collapses, the shared experiences and values that bind our communities together increasingly fragment. This fragmentation can lead to a sense of dislocation and alienation, weakening the bonds that hold societies together and making them more susceptible to division and conflict.

Economic Consequences

The economic consequences of a shrinking population are well-documented: reduced labor force participation, slower economic growth, and increased fiscal pressure on public services. However, these economic impacts also drive significant societal shifts. A stagnant or declining economy often leads to a sense of pessimism and fatalism, wherein individuals and communities feel that their best days have passed. This can have a self-reinforcing effect, further discouraging population growth and leading to a downward spiral of demographics and economy.

As economic opportunities diminish, young people are more likely to delay marriage and childbearing or to migrate to areas with better prospects. This migration can further the demographic challenges faced by certain regions, particularly rural, leading to a cycle of depopulation and decay. The loss of young people, who are often the most dynamic and innovative members of society, can stifle creativity and reduce the capacity for cultural renewal.

The economic pressures can lead to changes in values. As societies become more focused on economic survival, there is often a shift towards individualism and materialism, where personal success is prioritized over community and family. This shift can further undermine the cultural and social institutions that rely on a sense of collective responsibility and mutual support.

In response to declining birth rates, many Western nations have turned to immigration as a way to bolster their populations and sustain economic growth. While immigration can provide a temporary solution to fertility decline, it also introduces significant challenges. The integration of large numbers of immigrants, particularly when they come from diverse cultural backgrounds, can lead to tensions and conflicts as different cultural norms and values intersect.

The transformation brought about by immigration can be both enriching and destabilizing. On one hand, immigration can introduce new ideas, traditions, and perspectives, contributing to the cultural dynamism of a society. On the other hand, if not managed carefully, it can lead to the dissolution of national identity and social cohesion. When immigrant communities are not fully assimilated into the broader society, cultural enclaves can form, leading to parallel societies with distinct values and norms. This can create challenges for social unity and the maintenance of a shared cultural identity.

The reliance on immigration to address demographic this problem also raises questions about the sustainability of our traditions and values. If the native population continues to shrink, and if the cultural transmission mechanisms weaken, there is a risk that the core values and traditions that define us could be diluted or lost over time. This is not an argument against immigration per se, but rather a recognition of the complex cultural dynamics at play when demographic decline is addressed through population replacement rather than population renewal.

Politics and Geopolitics

The ramifications extend into the political realm as well. As populations shrink and age, political priorities often shift towards the interests of older generations, who tend to vote in greater numbers and have different concerns than younger people. This can lead to policies that are more focused on preserving the status quo and social programs rather than encouraging innovation and long-term growth.

The are also significant geopolitical concerns. Historically, population size and growth have been key drivers of national power and influence. As populations in the west, of traditional westerners decline relative to other regions, particularly in Asia and Africa, the global balance of power is likely to shift. This demographic reality could lead to a reduction in the ability to project power and influence on the world stage, with potentially destabilizing consequences for global order.

Immigration policies must be designed with an eye toward integration and cultural cohesion, ensuring that newcomers contribute to and strengthen the fabric of Western society rather than dilute it. However, the true measure of our success will be our ability to sustain ourselves demographically and culturally. The choices we make today will determine whether the West remains a vibrant, dynamic force in the world or fades into obscurity under the weight of its own decline.

The time for action is now. We stand at a crossroads where the future of Western civilization hangs in the balance. To preserve our way of life and ensure that our values endure, we must act decisively to renew our commitment to the principles that have made us strong. This is not just about numbers or policies—it is about the survival of a civilization that has shaped the modern world. We must seize this moment to renew, revitalize, and reclaim the future for ourselves and the generations to come.

4

The Immigration Illusion

Immigration as a Demographic Solution
The rationale behind using immigration to counteract demographic decline is straightforward: by bringing in younger, working-age individuals, countries can boost their labour force, maintain population levels, and ensure that there are enough workers to support an aging population. This approach is particularly appealing in countries where birth rates have fallen below the replacement level of 2.1 children per woman, leading to shrinking native populations and increased pressure on social welfare systems.

In theory, immigration can help stabilize population numbers and mitigate the economic impact of a declining birth rate. Immigrants, often younger and more willing to take on low-wage or labor-intensive jobs, can fill critical gaps in the workforce, especially in sectors like healthcare, construction, and agriculture, where native workers may be in short supply. Additionally, said immigrants theoretically contribute to the economy through their labour, consumption, and taxes, helping to sustain public services and support pension systems that are increasingly burdened by a growing number of retirees.

Proponents of immigration argue that it can enrich societies culturally and economically by bringing in diverse perspectives, and skills. In countries facing labor shortages and declining population, immigration is seen as a vital tool.

While immigration may provide some immediate benefits, it is not a sustainable solution to the underlying problems we are facing. Several key limitations undermine the effectiveness of immigration as a long-term demographic strategy:

The scale of demographic decline in many Western countries is so vast that even high levels of immigration cannot fully compensate for it. For example, countries like Japan, Italy, and Germany face significant population declines that would require unprecedented levels of immigration to offset. Such high levels of immigration may not be feasible or desirable, given the social, economic, and political challenges they entail.

Successfully integrating large numbers of immigrants into society is a complex and often difficult process. Language barriers, cultural differences, and varying levels of education and skills can hinder immigrants' ability to fully participate in the labour market and contribute. In some cases, poor integration leads to social tensions, segregation, and the rise of parallel communities, which accelerate social cohesion problems rather than solve them.

While immigrants can help fill labor shortages, there is also the potential for negative impacts on native workers, particularly in lower-skilled jobs. An influx of immigrant labor can suppress wages and increase competition for jobs, leading to resentment and social tension. This is particularly problematic in regions with high unemployment or where economic opportunities are limited, as native workers may perceive immigrants as a threat to their livelihoods.

The reliance on immigration as a demographic solution has led to significant political and social backlash in many Western countries. Concerns over national identity, culture, and the erosion of traditions have fuelled the rise of populist movements and anti-immigration sentiment. These movements have gained significant traction in recent years, leading to stricter immigration policies and a more polarized political landscape. This backlash complicates efforts to use immigration as a tool for demographic stabilization, as it becomes increasingly difficult to achieve broad public support for these policies.

Perhaps the most significant limitation of immigration as a solution is that it fails to address the root causes of declining birth rates and aging populations. Factors such as economic insecurity, housing affordability, work-life balance, and cultural attitudes towards family and child-rearing play a critical role in shaping demographic trends. Without addressing these underlying issues, the reliance on immigration is merely a stopgap measure that does nothing to encourage more babies.

Competency and Skills Gaps

The skills gap in Western economies is complicated, affecting both high-skilled and low-skilled sectors. On the one hand, there is a growing demand for workers with advanced technical skills, such as software development, engineering, data analysis, and healthcare specialties. On the other hand, there is also a shortage of workers willing to take on low-skilled jobs in industries such as agriculture, construction, and personal care, where native workers are either unavailable or unwilling to meet the demand.

Several factors contribute to the widening skills gap. Rapid advancements in technology have created demand for new skills, particularly in fields like information technology, cybersecurity, and advanced manufacturing. The pace of change is such that educational institutions and training programs struggle to keep up, leading to a shortage of workers with the necessary skills.

As the population ages, many experienced workers are retiring, leaving gaps in sectors where their expertise is difficult to replace. This is particularly acute in industries such as healthcare, where the demand for services is rising even as the workforce diminishes. There is a growing disconnect between the skills taught in educational institutions and those required in the labor market. Many graduates find that their degrees do not adequately prepare them for the jobs available, while employers report difficulties in finding candidates with the specific skills they need.

Given the growing skills gap, it is not surprising that Western countries have looked to immigration as a solution. The logic is straightforward: by bringing in workers from abroad, particularly those with specialized skills or the willingness to perform low-skilled labor, Western economies can mitigate the impact of the skills shortage. This assumption underlies many immigration policies that prioritize skilled workers or that encourage the migration of labor to sectors where domestic supply is lacking.

In some cases, this strategy has proven effective. High-skilled immigrants, particularly in the tech and healthcare sectors, have contributed significantly to innovation and have helped to address critical shortages. Similarly, low-skilled immigrants have taken on jobs in agriculture, construction, and service industries that are often shunned by native workers.

However, while immigration can provide some relief, it is not a comprehensive solution to the skills gap. The challenges associated with integrating immigrants into the labor market can be significant, and these challenges must be carefully managed if immigration is to contribute effectively to addressing the skills shortage.

Language is one of the most immediate and significant barriers that immigrants face when entering a new labor market. Proficiency in the local language is crucial for effective communication, particularly in high-skilled jobs where technical language and nuanced understanding are required. Language barriers can limit the ability of immigrants to fully integrate into the workplace, restrict their opportunities for advancement, and reduce their overall productivity. Even in low-skilled jobs, language barriers can lead to misunderstandings, safety issues, and difficulties in adhering to workplace standards.

The educational backgrounds of immigrants often differ significantly from those of native workers, and the quality of education varies widely across countries. Even when immigrants have the necessary qualifications, their credentials may not be recognized or valued in the host country. This can lead to underemployment, where highly skilled immigrants are forced to take jobs that do not utilize their full potential, or unemployment, where immigrants are unable to find work that matches their qualifications. The process of credential recognition can be time-consuming and costly, further hindering the ability of immigrants to contribute effectively to the labor market.

Cultural differences can also pose challenges to the integration of immigrants into the workforce. Workplace norms, expectations, and communication styles vary widely across cultures, and immigrants may struggle to adapt to these differences. In some cases, cultural misunderstandings can lead to conflicts, reduced workplace cohesion, and difficulties in building effective teams. Moreover, the experience of cultural isolation or discrimination can negatively impact the well-being and productivity of immigrant workers, making it harder for them to succeed in their new environment.

Beyond the workplace, the broader process of social and economic integration is critical to the success of immigrant workers. Access to affordable housing, education, healthcare, and social services plays a key role in determining how well immigrants can settle and contribute to their new communities. However, in many cases, immigrants face significant challenges in accessing these services, which can hinder their ability to fully participate in the labor market. Social integration is also important; immigrants who feel accepted and valued by the host society are more likely to be motivated and productive employees.

Policy and Structural Barriers

Immigration policies themselves can sometimes create barriers to integration. For example, temporary or seasonal work visas may limit the ability of immigrants to settle permanently and fully integrate into society. Similarly, restrictive policies around family reunification can prevent immigrants from bringing their families, which can lead to social isolation and reduce their overall well-being. Structural barriers within the labor market, such as discriminatory hiring practices or limited access to professional networks, can also hinder the successful integration of immigrants.

The impact of large-scale immigration extends far beyond the economic realm, influencing the cultural and social fabric of host societies. While immigration can bring cultural diversity and new perspectives, it also presents challenges that must be carefully managed to maintain social cohesion and ensure that communities remain strong and united. The influx of immigrants, particularly in large numbers, can lead to tensions between native populations and immigrant communities, as well as place significant strain on public services and infrastructure. Understanding these dynamics is essential for developing policies that promote harmony and integration, while also addressing the legitimate concerns of all citizens.

The tensions between native populations and immigrant communities can manifest in various ways, often reflecting underlying anxieties about economic competition, cultural differences, and social change. These tensions can be inflamed by several factors:

Economic Competition:

One of the most common sources of tension is the perception that immigrants are competing with native workers for jobs, housing, and other resources. This is particularly pronounced in low-skilled labor markets, where the influx of immigrant workers can suppress wages and increase competition for employment. In regions with high unemployment or economic insecurity, this can lead to resentment and hostility towards immigrants, who are seen as taking jobs away from native workers.

Cultural Misunderstandings:

Cultural differences can lead to misunderstandings and conflicts between native populations and immigrant communities. These misunderstandings can arise from differences in language, social norms, religious practices, and communication styles. When such differences are not adequately addressed through dialogue and education, they can contribute to stereotypes, prejudice, and discrimination, further deepening the divide between communities.

Crime and Security Concerns:

The perception that immigrants are associated with higher levels of crime can also fuel tensions. While research shows that crime rates among immigrants are generally similar to or lower than those of native populations, isolated incidents or sensationalized media coverage can create a perception of insecurity. This can lead to calls for tougher immigration policies and increased law enforcement in immigrant communities, which in turn can exacerbate feelings of marginalization and resentment.

Political and Media Influence:

The way immigration is framed in political discourse and the media plays a significant role in shaping public attitudes. Politicians and media outlets that emphasize the negative aspects of immigration, such as economic burdens or cultural clashes, can inflame tensions and contribute to a polarized environment. Conversely, positive portrayals of immigrant contributions can help to reduce tensions and promote a more inclusive society.

The Strain on Public Services and Infrastructure

Large-scale immigration also places significant demands on public services and infrastructure, which can lead to challenges in service delivery and exacerbate existing inequalities. The strain on these systems can contribute to tensions between native populations and immigrants, particularly when resources are perceived to be scarce or unevenly distributed.

Healthcare Services:

The arrival of large numbers of immigrants can increase demand for healthcare services, particularly in regions that are already experiencing shortages of medical professionals or facilities. This can lead to longer wait times, reduced access to care, and increased pressure on healthcare providers. In some cases, native populations may perceive that immigrants are receiving preferential treatment or straining the system, leading to resentment.

Education:

Schools in areas with high levels of immigration may face challenges in accommodating students with diverse linguistic and cultural backgrounds. This can require additional resources for language instruction, cultural integration programs, and support services, which may be in short supply. When educational resources are stretched thin, it can lead to tensions between parents, students, and educators, particularly if native students are perceived to be disadvantaged by the influx of immigrant children.

Housing and Infrastructure:

The demand for housing and infrastructure often increases with large-scale immigration, putting pressure on available resources. In cities and regions with limited housing stock, this can lead to rising rents and housing shortages, which disproportionately affect low-income residents. Infrastructure such as transportation, utilities, and public spaces may also become overburdened, leading to congestion, deterioration, and reduced quality of life. When native populations perceive that immigrants are contributing to these problems, it can fuel opposition to immigration policies.

Welfare and Social Services:

Immigrants may require access to social services such as unemployment benefits, childcare, and social housing, particularly during the initial period of settlement. This can increase the strain on welfare systems, which may already be under pressure due to aging populations and economic challenges. Native populations may resent the allocation of resources to immigrants, particularly if they believe that their own needs are not being adequately met.

The cultural and social impact of large-scale immigration is complex, influencing everything from social cohesion to the capacity of public services and infrastructure. While immigration can bring many benefits, it also presents challenges that must be carefully managed to ensure that the positive aspects outweigh the negative.

To address these challenges, policymakers must take a holistic approach that considers the needs of both native populations and immigrant communities. This includes investing in integration programs that promote cultural understanding and encouraging open dialogue to address the concerns of all citizens.

Ultimately, the success of immigration policies depends on their ability to balance the benefits of diversity with the need for shared values. By addressing the cultural and social impacts of immigration, Western societies can build stronger communities that are capable of navigating the complexities of a globalized world.

5

The Death of the Trades

The Rise and Fall of Skilled Labor

Skilled labor, encompassing a wide range of trades such as carpentry, plumbing, electrical work, masonry, and metalworking, has been the backbone of Western civilization's development. From the industrial revolution to the modern era, tradesmen have been instrumental in constructing the infrastructure, homes, and industries that have driven economic growth and progress. However, in recent decades, the value and prevalence of skilled labor have declined sharply, contributing to a widening skills gap and a shift away from the appreciation of manual work. Understanding the historical context of skilled labor's rise and its subsequent decline is crucial to addressing the challenges facing the West today.

The rise of skilled labor can be traced back to the early stages of Western civilization, particularly during the Middle Ages and the Renaissance, when the development of trade guilds laid the foundation for what would become the modern trades. These guilds were associations of craftsmen and artisans who regulated the practice of their trades and maintained quality standards while providing training to apprentices. Guilds played a crucial role in the economic and social fabric of medieval cities, ensuring that skilled labor was recognized and passed down through generations.

The importance of the trades became even more pronounced during the Industrial Revolution, which began in the late 18th century. As

Western nations transitioned from agrarian economies to industrial powerhouses, the demand for skilled tradesmen skyrocketed. The construction of factories, railways, bridges, and urban centres required a vast workforce of skilled labourers who could operate machinery, build complex structures, and maintain the rapidly expanding infrastructure.

Not only was this the foundation of industrialization but also a key driver of innovation. Many of the technological advancements of the 19th and early 20th centuries were the result of skilled workers applying their expertise to solve practical problems. The development of steam engines, electrical systems, manufacturing processes, and many more, relied heavily on the knowledge and craftsmanship of these workers.

The post-World War II era saw a continuation of this trend, playing a critical role in the reconstruction of Europe and the expansion of the American economy. The construction boom of the 1950s and 1960s, driven by suburbanization and the growth of the middle class, created a high demand for tradespeople. Skilled labor was not only abundant but also well-respected, with tradesmen enjoying stable, well-paying jobs that provided a pathway to upward mobility.

Shifts in Education and Culture

Despite its historical importance, skilled labor has experienced a sharp decline in recent decades, both in terms of its value and its prevalence within the workforce. This decline can be attributed to several interrelated factors, including shifts in education and cultural attitudes.

One of the most significant factors contributing to the decline is the shift in educational priorities. Beginning in the latter half of the 20th century, we increasingly emphasized higher education as the primary pathway to success. The narrative that a four-year college degree was the key to a prosperous future became dominant, leading to the devaluation of vocational and technical education. High schools began to phase out shop classes and vocational programs, and students were encouraged to pursue academic degrees, regardless of their interests or aptitudes.

This shift had major consequences for the labour market. As more young people pursued college degrees, fewer entered the trades, leading to a growing skills gap in industries that rely on skilled labor. At the same time, the overemphasis on higher education led to an oversupply of college graduates in fields that did not align with market demands, resulting in underemployment and a devaluation of certain degrees. The push for universal college education, while well-intentioned, contributed to a cultural perception that skilled trades were less prestigious or desirable than white-collar professions.

Cultural attitudes towards manual labor also played a role in the decline of the trades. As Western societies became more affluent, there was a growing disconnect between the consumer culture that relied on goods and services and the labor required to produce them. Skilled tradesmen, once seen as the backbone of the economy, were increasingly viewed as part of the working class—a group often stigmatized or overlooked in favour of professions perceived as more intellectual or prestigious. This shift in perception contributed to a decline in respect, further discouraging young people from pursuing careers.

Economic changes also contributed to the decline of the trades. The globalization of the economy, which accelerated in the late 20th century, led to the offshoring of many manufacturing jobs to countries with lower labor costs. This shift not only reduced the demand for skilled labor in Western nations but also contributed to the dismantling of entire industries that had once provided stable employment for tradespeople.

Technological advancements, while often beneficial, also played a role. Automation and the rise of computer-aided manufacturing reduced the need for certain types of manual labour, leading to job losses in some trades. While technology created new opportunities in fields like robotics and advanced manufacturing, these jobs often required different skill sets, leaving traditional tradesmen behind.

The rise of the gig economy and the shift towards contract and temporary work undermined the stability and benefits that had traditionally been associated with skilled trades. Many found themselves working in precarious conditions, with less job security, fewer benefits, and lower wages than in previous generations.

Consequences

One of the most immediate impacts has been the widening skills gap in industries that are essential to the functioning of modern economies. Construction, manufacturing, and infrastructure maintenance all rely on a steady supply of skilled tradesmen, yet many of these industries are now facing severe shortages. This skills gap not only slows economic growth but also drives up costs and leads to delays in critical projects.

As the availability of stable, well-paying jobs in the trades has diminished, many workers have been left with few viable career options. This has particularly impacted working-class communities, where the trades were once a pathway to middle-class stability. The loss of these opportunities has contributed to the economic disenfranchisement of large segments of the population, accelerating social and economic divides.

We have also found a growing disconnect between the production of goods and the people who create them. The devaluation of manual work has contributed to a broader shift towards consumerism, where the focus is on the consumption of goods rather than the craftsmanship and labor that go into their creation. This disconnect has further marginalized the trades, reducing their visibility and diminishing their significance.

As vocational and technical education programs have been phased out, students who might have excelled in them are left with fewer options. This has contributed to higher dropout rates, underemployment, and a loss of opportunities for upward mobility for those who do not pursue higher education.

The Intellectual Elite vs. Practical Skills:

In the modern world, the dichotomy between intellectualism and practical skills has become increasingly pronounced. Over the past several decades, our society has placed an ever-growing emphasis on intellectual achievement—academic credentials, theoretical knowledge, and abstract thinking while simultaneously devaluing the practical skills that are essential to maintaining and advancing the physical world we live in. This glorification of intellectualism has further marginalized trade work.

The rise of the intellectual elite in the West can be traced back to the post-World War II era, when higher education became increasingly accessible and valued. Governments and educational institutions promoted the idea that a college degree was the key to personal and professional success, leading to a significant expansion of universities and a surge in the number of people pursuing higher education. The introduction of "for profit" colleges and universities added ever increasing fuel to the fire. The intellectual elite, comprising academics, professionals, and thought leaders, became the standard-bearers of societal progress. Their work in the sciences, humanities, and social sciences was seen as the driving force behind innovation and policy.

As a result, the pursuit of intellectualism became not just a personal goal but an expectation. Success was defined by the attainment of advanced degrees, prestigious academic positions, and recognition. This emphasis created a cultural hierarchy in which those engaged in practical, manual work were seen as occupying a lower rung on the social ladder.

As society placed greater value on intellectual pursuits, trade work—carpentry, plumbing, electrical work, and other skilled trades—began to be viewed as less important and desirable. This marginalization was reflected in the education system, where vocational training programs were gradually phased out in favour of academic curricula. High schools that once offered robust trade programs began to shift their focus toward college preparation and standardized testing. Students who were more inclined toward hands-on, practical work were often discouraged from pursuing careers in the trades. Instead, they were pushed toward academic paths.

The result was a growing disconnect between the educational system and the needs of the labor market. As more students pursued college degrees, fewer entered the trades, leading to a skills shortage in industries that rely on skilled labor. This shortage was furthered by the perception that trade work was a "second-class" occupation, suitable only for those who could not succeed in more desirable pursuits.

In a world increasingly dominated by digital technology and virtual experiences, the tangible, hands-on work of the tradesman has become less visible and less valued. The result is a society that is disconnected from the physical world and the ability to build and maintain is taken for granted, while the people who perform these essential tasks are often overlooked.

The Skills Shortage

We are now entering a major skills shortage in Western countries, particularly in industries such as construction, manufacturing, and infrastructure maintenance. This shortage is not just a matter of inconvenience; it is a crisis that threatens the sustainability of the economy and the quality of life for millions of people.

In the construction industry, for example, the shortage of skilled trades has led to significant delays and cost overruns on major projects. Buildings, roads, and infrastructure projects that are critical to the growth and safety of the public are often stalled due to a lack of qualified workers. The shortage of electricians, plumbers, carpenters, and other trades means that repairs and maintenance are often deferred, leading to deteriorating infrastructure and increasing the risk of accidents and failures.

The manufacturing sector, once the backbone of Western economies, has also been hit hard. As older generations retire, there are not enough young people to replace them. This has led to a decline in productivity and innovation, as companies struggle to find the experience necessary to operate advanced machinery and maintain production lines.

The skills shortage also has significant economic implications. As demand outstrips supply, wages for these positions have risen, making it more expensive for businesses to hire and retain qualified workers. This, in turn, drives up the cost of goods and services, contributing to inflation and reducing our competitiveness on the global stage.

The devaluation of trade work has fuelled a growing sense of alienation and disenfranchisement among those who rely on these jobs to make a living. As globalization shifted manufacturing overseas, regions like the Rust Belt were left decimated, stripping entire communities of purpose leading to the rise of addiction in these economically gutted areas. This divide not only widens the gap between the elite and the working class but also exacerbates ongoing skills shortages, leaving the next generation with little incentive to enter a field seen as undervalued and unstable.

As the number of skilled tradespeople dwindles, the effects ripple through the economy, causing significant disruptions in key sectors and threatening the stability and growth. The loss of skilled labor not only slows down economic development but also undermines the very foundations of modern life, leading to a host of challenges that affect everything from the construction of buildings to the maintenance of essential services.

Infrastructure—roads, bridges, power grids, water systems, and telecommunications networks—is the backbone of any modern economy. The construction and maintenance of this infrastructure depend heavily on skilled tradesmen. However, the decline in trade work has led to a severe shortage of these professionals, which in turn has created a host of problems for infrastructure projects. One of the most immediate consequences is the delay and increased cost of infrastructure projects. Construction timelines are extended, and the cost of labor rises. These delays and cost overruns have become a common feature of infrastructure development. Projects that are essential for economic growth, such as the expansion of highways, the modernization of airports, and the upgrading of power grids, are often stalled or scaled back due to the lack of available workers and increasingly, expertise.

Many Western countries are grappling with aging infrastructure that requires constant maintenance and repair. Bridges, roads, water systems, and electrical grids that were built decades ago are now in urgent need of upgrades. The consequences of such failures can be devastating, resulting in significant disruptions to daily life and even death.

Poor infrastructure reduces productivity, increasing the cost of doing business and making regions less attractive for investment. Companies rely on efficient transportation networks, reliable power supplies, and robust communication systems to operate effectively. When these systems are compromised due to a lack of skill, businesses suffer.

The Impact on Industry

In manufacturing, the shortage has led to decreased productivity and a loss of competitiveness. Manufacturing processes often require precise and specialized skills, such as welding, machining, and electrical work. Without a sufficient number of skilled workers, factories struggle to meet production targets, leading to delays and lower quality products, while driving up costs. This decline in manufacturing capability has contributed to the offshoring of jobs to countries where skilled labor is more readily available, further collapsing the industrial base of Western economies.

The energy sector is also feeling the impact. The operation and maintenance of power plants, oil refineries, and renewable energy installations require a highly skilled workforce. As the number of tradesmen declines, energy companies are finding it increasingly difficult to maintain their infrastructure and meet the growing demand for energy. This has led to concerns about the reliability of energy supplies and the ability to improve and expand existing energy sources.

The most obvious impact is on the availability and cost of services. Electricians, plumbers, and HVAC technicians, are essential for maintaining homes and businesses. As their numbers decline, the cost of these services increases, and wait times for repairs and installations grow longer. This can be particularly problematic in emergencies, where a delay in service can lead to significant damage or discomfort.

For example, a shortage of plumbers means that homeowners may have to wait days or even weeks to fix a broken pipe, leading to water damage and costly repairs. Similarly, a lack of HVAC technicians can leave homes and businesses without heating or cooling during extreme weather conditions, posing health risks and reducing quality of life.

As trade work has been devalued, fewer young people are entering the trades, leading to a lack of training and apprenticeship opportunities. This has created a vicious cycle where the skills shortage perpetuates itself, making it increasingly difficult to address the underlying issues. The lack of investment in education and training means that young people are missing out on stable, well-paying career opportunities in the trades, furthering the economic divide between those with academic degrees and those with practical skills. In a society that increasingly values intellectual achievement over practical skills, there is a loss of appreciation for the craftsmanship.

To reverse the problem, society must rethink how it values trade work. The current shortage of skilled labor is not just an economic problem—it's a cultural failure that is already slowing infrastructure development and increasing the cost of essential services. The impacts of this neglect are evident in daily life, from higher costs to longer wait times and diminished access to critical services.

Revitalizing vocational education is a necessary first step. Schools must provide robust trade programs that offer students real-world skills and the chance to pursue rewarding careers. Outdated curricula must be updated to meet the needs of today's workforce, and trades should be presented as honourable, rewarding professions, not as fallback options.

We must challenge the belief that intellectual achievement is the only marker of success. It's time to celebrate the expertise, creativity, and craftsmanship that tradespeople bring to their work. Public campaigns, media representation, and community initiatives can elevate the status of trade work, inspiring more young people to consider these paths.

Policies that support the trades are essential. Businesses must be incentivized to invest in apprenticeships and training, and the trades deserve competitive wages and benefits that reflect the importance of their work. Ensuring that trade work is not only viable but respected and well-compensated is critical to reversing the current decline.

Finally, the false divide between intellectual and manual work must be broken. Both are necessary for a functioning society, and neither should be considered superior to the other. By developing a culture that values both, we can ensure that practical skills are not only preserved but also enhanced by technological innovation.

6

Envy and Entitlement

I n the past, Western culture was driven by a spirit of ambition, where individuals were encouraged to strive for excellence, innovate, and achieve great things. Ambition was seen as a virtue and brought about progress and prosperity. However, in recent decades, this cultural narrative has shifted dramatically. Envy, once considered a base emotion to be overcome, has been weaponized and has become a pervasive force in Western society. This "cult of envy" has turned ambition into something suspect, even punishable, and has had a corrosive effect on both individual initiative and societal progress.

The Rise of Envy as a Cultural Force

Envy is an emotion as old as humanity itself, but its elevation to a central cultural force is a relatively recent phenomenon. In traditional Western thought, envy was regarded as one of the seven deadly sins, a destructive emotion that led to bitterness, and resentment. It was seen as something to be avoided, an obstacle to personal growth and social harmony.

However, as Western societies became more egalitarian and as the ideals of fairness and equality gained prominence, envy began to be recast in a different light. In a world where equality of outcome was increasingly emphasized over equality of opportunity, the success of others began to be seen less as a result of merit and more as a product of privilege or exploitation. This shift in perspective laid the groundwork for the weaponization of envy, where the achievements of the ambitious became targets for social and political retribution.

The rise of social media has further amplified this phenomenon. Platforms that allow individuals to share their successes and lifestyles with a global audience have inadvertently fuelled the flames of envy. Constant exposure to the curated images of others' successes—whether real or exaggerated—has made it easier for envy to take root. The ability to compare oneself to others on a massive scale has created a breeding ground for resentment, where the success of others is seen not as something to aspire to but as something to begrudge.

The Demonization of Ambition

As envy has taken hold, ambition—once celebrated as the engine of progress—has come under attack. Ambitious individuals, particularly those who achieve significant success, are increasingly viewed with suspicion. Their accomplishments are often scrutinized, not for what they contribute to society, but for what they allegedly take away from others. This shift in perception has turned ambition from a virtue into a vice, something to be punished rather than admired.

This demonization of ambition is evident in various spheres of life. In the corporate world, successful entrepreneurs and business leaders are often portrayed as villains who have amassed wealth and power at the expense of others. Their success is frequently attributed to exploitation, luck, or unfair advantage, rather than to hard work, innovation, or talent. This narrative is reinforced by media portrayals and political rhetoric that frame wealth and success as inherently suspect, feeding into the idea that those who succeed must have done so at the cost of the less fortunate.

In academia and intellectual circles, the cult of envy manifests in the rejection of meritocracy. The idea that individuals should rise based on their abilities and efforts has increasingly come under fire as being inherently unfair. The focus has shifted from rewarding excellence to ensuring that no one feels left behind, even if it means lowering standards and punishing those who excel. This has led to the rise of policies and practices that prioritize equality of outcome over excellence, further marginalizing the ambitious and discouraging the pursuit of greatness.

The demonization is also evident in the political sphere, where populist movements have gained traction by tapping into the envy and resentment of those who feel left behind by globalization and economic change. Politicians who promise to "take down the elites" or "redistribute wealth" often do so by appealing to the base emotions of envy, turning the success of others into a rallying cry for retribution. This has led to policies that penalize success—through higher taxes, stricter regulations, and wealth redistribution—under the guise of fairness and social justice.

The weaponization of envy has far-reaching consequences, both at the individual and collective levels. At the individual level, the demonization of ambition creates a culture of mediocrity, where striving for excellence is discouraged and where the pursuit of success is seen as inherently selfish or harmful. This cultural shift stifles innovation and creativity, as individuals become less willing to take risks, push boundaries, or stand out from the crowd.

The cult of envy also undermines social cohesion. Rather than fostering a sense of shared purpose and collective progress, it creates division and resentment. Envy breeds a zero-sum mentality, where the success of one person is seen as a loss for others, leading to social fragmentation and conflict. This erosion of social trust makes it more difficult to build and sustain the institutions that are necessary for a healthy, functioning society.

Economically, the consequences of weaponizing envy are equally damaging. By punishing ambition and success, societies risk driving away the very individuals who are capable of creating jobs, generating wealth, and driving economic growth. When entrepreneurs and innovators are discouraged or penalized, they are less likely to invest in new ventures, less likely to create new technologies, and less likely to contribute to the overall prosperity of society. This can lead to economic stagnation, reduced competitiveness, and a decline in living standards.

The weaponization of envy also has political consequences. As envy becomes a driving force in political discourse, it can lead to the rise of populist leaders who exploit these emotions for their own gain. Such leaders often promise to level the playing field by punishing the successful, but in doing so, they create policies that undermine economic freedom, reduce incentives for innovation, and stifle economic growth. This can result in a vicious cycle where economic decline feeds further envy and resentment, leading to more punitive policies and deeper social divisions.

Entitlement Culture

In the past, the Western world was defined by a strong work ethic—a cultural cornerstone that emphasized diligence, responsibility, and the belief that success was earned through hard work and perseverance. This ethic was the driving force behind the industrial and technological advancements that propelled Western societies to unprecedented heights of prosperity and influence. However, in recent decades, a pervasive sense of entitlement has taken root, gradually eroding this once-strong work ethic. This entitlement culture, which fosters the expectation of rewards without effort, has led to a generation that is increasingly unprepared for the challenges of the real world, with significant implications for both individuals and society as a whole.

The rise of entitlement culture can be traced to a combination of social, economic, and educational factors that have reshaped the expectations and attitudes of younger generations. Central to this shift is the growing belief that success and comfort are not something to be earned, but something to be expected as a birthright.

One of the key contributors to this cultural shift is the expansion of the welfare state and the increasing availability of social safety nets.

While these systems were originally designed to provide support for those in need, they have, in some cases, created a dependency that undermines the motivation to work and strive for self-sufficiency. The availability of unemployment benefits, housing assistance, and other forms of government support has, for some, reduced the perceived necessity of finding and maintaining steady employment. This has led to a sense of entitlement to a certain standard of living, regardless of one's effort or contribution to society.

In addition to the welfare state, the education system has played a significant role in fostering entitlement culture. Over the past several decades, there has been a shift in educational philosophy from one that emphasizes competition and excellence to one that prioritizes inclusivity and self-esteem. This shift has led to the widespread adoption of practices such as grade inflation, the elimination of failing grades, and the de-emphasis of merit-based achievement. As a result, many students graduate with inflated perceptions of their abilities and an expectation of success that is disconnected from their actual skills and efforts.

Furthermore, the rise of "helicopter parenting" and the overprotection of children have contributed to the development of entitlement attitudes. Parents who shield their children from failure, hardship, and the consequences of their actions inadvertently teach them that they are entitled to success without effort. This overprotective parenting style has led to a generation of young adults who are ill-equipped to handle the challenges and setbacks that are an inevitable part of life.

The sense of entitlement that has become pervasive in Western culture has fundamentally undermined the work ethic that once defined these societies. When individuals believe that they are entitled to success, comfort, and recognition without having to work for them, the motivation to put in the necessary effort diminishes. This has led to a widespread decline in the values of hard work, perseverance, and personal responsibility.

In the workplace, this entitlement mentality manifests in several ways. Employers increasingly report that younger workers often expect promotions, raises, and accolades without demonstrating the necessary performance or dedication. There is a growing trend of job-hopping, where individuals leave positions quickly when their expectations are not immediately met, rather than investing time and effort into building a career. This lack of commitment and perseverance undermines both individual career development and the stability of organizations.

The decline in work ethic is also evident in educational settings, where students increasingly expect high grades and academic success with minimal effort. The emphasis on self-esteem and the avoidance of failure have led to a culture where students are rewarded simply for participation, rather than for actual achievement. This has resulted in a generation of graduates who are unprepared for the demands of the workforce, where effort, resilience, and the ability to overcome challenges are crucial to success.

Moreover, the entitlement mentality has contributed to a broader societal shift away from the values of self-reliance and personal responsibility. When individuals believe that they are owed certain benefits or rewards, they are less likely to take responsibility for their own lives and well-being. This has led to a decline in the willingness to engage in difficult or unglamorous work, and a growing expectation that others—whether employers, the government, or society at large—should provide for their needs.

The rise of entitlement culture has far-reaching consequences for both individuals and society. At the individual level, those who are raised with a sense of entitlement are often ill-prepared for the realities of the world. When they encounter challenges, setbacks, or failures, they are more likely to become discouraged or disengaged, rather than persisting and overcoming obstacles. This lack of resilience and adaptability can lead to chronic underachievement, dissatisfaction, and a sense of disillusionment.

Furthermore, the entitlement mentality can lead to strained relationships, both in the workplace and in personal life. Individuals who expect others to cater to their needs without reciprocating effort or support often find themselves isolated or resented by those around them. In the workplace, this can result in conflicts with colleagues or supervisors, reduced teamwork and collaboration, and ultimately, a lack of career advancement.

At the societal level, entitlement culture undermines the very principles that have driven Western success—namely, the belief in hard work, personal responsibility, and the pursuit of excellence. As the work ethic declines, so too does productivity, innovation, and economic growth. Industries that rely on skilled, dedicated workers struggle to find and retain talent, leading to labor shortages, decreased efficiency, and reduced competitiveness on the global stage.

Additionally, the erosion of the work ethic contributes to economic inequality and social division. Those who succeed through hard work and determination may become increasingly resentful of those who expect rewards without effort, leading to a widening gap between the industrious and the entitled. This divide can fuel social tensions and undermine the cohesion and stability of communities.

Envy, the resentful awareness of another's advantages and the desire to possess them, has always been a destructive force in human relations. However, in contemporary Western society, envy has been weaponized and institutionalized, transforming from a personal vice into a collective cultural norm. This shift has profound implications for the moral integrity of society.

Envy erodes the moral fabric by turning the focus away from self-improvement and the pursuit of excellence, directing it instead toward the devaluation of others' successes. In a culture dominated by envy, the achievements of individuals are not celebrated as examples to emulate but are instead viewed as unfair advantages that must be leveled or taken away. This mindset fosters a zero-sum view of the world, where one person's success is perceived as a direct threat to another's, leading to a cultural landscape rife with resentment and hostility.

The impact of envy on societal values is profound. Instead of encouraging individuals to aspire to greater heights, envy drives a desire to bring others down. This creates a culture of mediocrity, where those who excel are often punished rather than rewarded. In workplaces, schools, and communities, the fear of inciting envy can lead individuals to hide their successes or underplay their achievements, stifling innovation and discouraging the pursuit of excellence. As a result, the moral imperative to strive for personal and collective betterment is replaced by a desire to conform to the lowest common denominator, ensuring that no one stands out too much or achieves too much.

While envy poisons the relationship between individuals, entitlement corrodes the individual's relationship with society. Entitlement is the belief that one is inherently deserving of privileges or special treatment without having to earn them. This mentality has taken root in Western culture, leading to a widespread erosion of the values of hard work, responsibility, and accountability.

Entitlement undermines the moral fabric of society by creating a disconnect between effort and reward. When individuals believe they are owed success, wealth, or recognition simply by virtue of their existence, the incentive to work hard, innovate, or take responsibility for one's actions diminishes. This leads to a culture where mediocrity is not just tolerated but expected, as there is little motivation to go beyond the minimum effort required.

The sense of entitlement also leads to a breakdown in the social contract, the implicit agreement between individuals and society that one must contribute in order to receive benefits. When entitlement prevails, this contract is inverted: individuals demand benefits without feeling obligated to contribute in return. This has far-reaching consequences for societal cohesion and economic productivity, as the collective effort needed to sustain and improve society is undermined by a growing expectation of unearned rewards.

Moreover, entitlement breeds a culture of victimhood, where individuals and groups increasingly identify themselves as oppressed or disadvantaged, demanding redress not through their own efforts but through the redistribution of others' success. This fosters a grievance mentality, where the focus shifts from what one can achieve through hard work to what one can extract from society by claiming victim status. This mentality erodes personal accountability and stifles the entrepreneurial spirit, further entrenching mediocrity as the norm.

The combined forces of envy and entitlement have created a cultural environment where excellence is increasingly suppressed. In such an environment, those who achieve great things—whether through innovation, creativity, or sheer hard work—are often viewed with suspicion or resentment. Their successes are attributed not to their efforts or abilities but to privilege, luck, or exploitation. This narrative not only devalues individual achievement but also discourages others from striving for excellence, as the rewards for doing so are diminished by the backlash of envy and the demands of entitlement.

The suppression of excellence has dire consequences for society. In education, the pressure to ensure equal outcomes for all students has led to the lowering of academic standards and the devaluation of merit. Rather than challenging students to reach their full potential, the focus has shifted to ensuring that no one feels left behind, even if it means holding back the most talented and ambitious. This has resulted in a generation of young people who are ill-prepared for the demands of the real world, lacking the skills and resilience needed to succeed in a competitive environment.

In the workplace, the erosion of excellence manifests in the rise of mediocrity. As organizations prioritize inclusivity and equality of outcome over meritocracy and performance, the incentive to excel is weakened. Promotions, raises, and recognition are increasingly based on factors other than merit, leading to a workforce that is less motivated, less innovative, and less productive. This decline in work ethic and performance has long-term consequences for economic growth, competitiveness, and overall societal prosperity.

The cultural shift away from excellence also affects the broader society. When mediocrity is normalized and excellence is suppressed, the collective aspiration to achieve great things is lost. This leads to a stagnation of progress, where society is content to maintain the status quo rather than push the boundaries of what is possible. In such a society, innovation slows, creativity diminishes, and the drive to solve the complex challenges of the future is weakened.

The moral decay resulting from the rise of envy and entitlement is evident in the way these forces have reshaped societal values. In a culture where mediocrity thrives and excellence is suppressed, the virtues of hard work, perseverance, and personal responsibility are increasingly devalued. Instead, society celebrates those who demand the most while contributing the least, rewarding grievance over grit and victimhood over victory.

This moral decay has significant implications for the future of Western civilization. As the foundations of hard work, merit, and excellence are eroded, the ability of society to sustain itself and progress is compromised. The decline in moral standards leads to a decline in social cohesion, as individuals and groups become more focused on their own entitlements and grievances than on the collective good. This fragmentation of society weakens the bonds that hold communities together, leading to increased polarization, conflict, and instability.

Furthermore, the moral decay undermines the legitimacy of institutions and the rule of law. When society is governed by envy and entitlement, the principles of fairness, justice, and equality of opportunity are replaced by demands for equality of outcome, regardless of effort or merit. This shift erodes trust in institutions, as they are increasingly seen as instruments of redistribution rather than as protectors of rights and enablers of progress. The result is a loss of faith in the very structures that are essential for the functioning of a stable and prosperous society.

To counter the moral decay caused by envy and entitlement, Western societies must undergo a cultural renewal that re-emphasizes the values of hard work, personal responsibility, and the pursuit of excellence. This renewal must begin with a rejection of the zero-sum mentality that views the success of others as a threat and instead embraces the idea that individual achievement contributes to the collective good.

Education plays a critical role in this renewal. Schools and universities must return to a focus on merit and excellence, challenging students to reach their full potential and rewarding those who excel. This requires a shift away from the current emphasis on inclusivity at the expense of standards and a recommitment to the principles of competition and achievement. By cultivating a culture of excellence in education, society can prepare the next generation to take on the challenges of the future with confidence and capability.

In the workplace, organizations must reestablish meritocracy as the guiding principle for hiring, promotion, and recognition. This means rewarding performance, innovation, and dedication, rather than prioritizing diversity quotas or appeasing the demands of entitlement. By creating an environment where excellence is valued and mediocrity is not tolerated, businesses can drive innovation, increase productivity, and contribute to economic growth.

At the societal level, there must be a renewed emphasis on the importance of personal responsibility and self-reliance. This involves promoting the idea that success is earned through hard work and perseverance, not given as a right. Public discourse, media representation, and community initiatives can play a role in reshaping cultural attitudes, encouraging individuals to take ownership of their lives and to strive for greatness.

Finally, political leaders must resist the temptation to exploit envy and entitlement for short-term gains. Instead, they should promote policies that encourage innovation, reward hard work, and create opportunities for all individuals to achieve their potential. By fostering a culture that values merit and excellence, political leaders can help to restore the moral fabric of society and ensure that Western civilization continues to thrive.

7

The Welfare State

As we've seen in the collapse of the trades, the erosion of personal responsibility has been systematically encouraged by the state's involvement in every aspect of our lives. What was once a people driven by ingenuity and hard work has become one weighed down by handouts and the seductive grip of the welfare state.

The Origins of the Welfare State
The welfare state didn't emerge overnight. It began as a well-intentioned response to the hardships of the Great Depression, when social safety nets were designed to help those who had fallen through the cracks. But as with any government intervention, what began as a small, targeted program ballooned into a leviathan. Today, the welfare state encompasses every aspect of life, from healthcare to housing, from unemployment benefits to child subsidies. Each expansion is justified by some noble cause, but the result is the same: greater dependency and less individual responsibility.

The state was never meant to provide lifelong support to able-bodied individuals. But somewhere along the way, the line between temporary aid and permanent reliance was blurred. Now, it's not just the truly needy who rely on the state, but a growing class of individuals who have learned to game the system, demanding more and more from a government that seems only too willing to oblige.

Devaluation of the Dollar

The economic consequences of the welfare state are staggering, and one of the most glaring is the devaluation of the dollar. Since the United States abandoned the gold standard in 1971, we have seen an explosion in the money supply. With fiat currency, the value of money is no longer tied to a finite resource like gold but is instead based on trust—trust that the government won't inflate the currency into oblivion. Unfortunately, that trust has been broken time and again.

In the last 50 years, the dollar has lost over 85% of its purchasing power. That's not just a number—it's a reflection of the real-world consequences of reckless monetary policy. When the government prints money to fund its endless welfare programs, the value of every dollar in circulation decreases. What does that mean for the average person? It means higher prices for goods and services, stagnant wages, and a lower standard of living, sound familiar? While promising to help those in need, it ironically does the most damage to the very people it claims to support.

Take inflation as a concrete example. In 2023, inflation surged to over 6%, far above the government's target of 2%. This was largely driven by massive government spending, including trillions in welfare and stimulus programs. The result? An average household lost nearly $4,000 in purchasing power over the course of the year. For those on fixed incomes, particularly welfare recipients, this erosion of the dollar's value has a devastating impact. Yet, the government's response is always more welfare, more spending, and more of the very policies that are causing the problem.

The Tax Burden

To fund this bloated welfare state, the government must constantly raise taxes. In 2022, the average American paid over 30% of their income in taxes, a number that continues to climb each year. This includes federal income tax, state and local taxes, payroll taxes, and countless hidden taxes on goods and services. While politicians love to talk about taxing the rich, the reality is that the burden falls disproportionately on the middle class, who see their hard-earned money siphoned away to fund programs that they may never benefit from.

What's worse is how this tax revenue is used. A significant portion goes not toward productive investments like infrastructure or education but toward sustaining a bloated bureaucracy rife with inefficiency and corruption. In 2023, the U.S. government spent $6.27 trillion, with over 40% of that going toward various forms of welfare, including healthcare subsidies, social security, and unemployment benefits. And while the welfare rolls continue to expand, so too does the level of corruption.

In the midst of a crumbling Western economy, plagued by soaring inflation, a devalued currency, and a welfare state draining its productivity, we have witnessed an astonishing amount of resources funnelled into Ukraine. Western nations, particularly the United States and European Union, have allocated billions in military aid, humanitarian assistance, and financial support. The justification? A war on the other side of the world, framed as a fight for democracy. Yet, while these funds flow abroad, cities at home crumble, infrastructure remains neglected, and social programs balloon beyond sustainability.

It's a staggering contradiction: the very governments advocating for ever-increasing taxes to fund their broken welfare systems are the same ones handing over resources to a foreign conflict, with little accountability for how it's spent. The result is a growing public discontent, as citizens see their hard-earned dollars redirected away from their own streets and into a proxy war. This siphoning of wealth is a hallmark of the Western decline—an empire propping up foreign interests while letting its own decay from within. If this isn't symptomatic of an elite-driven agenda, then what is?

It's no secret that welfare programs are rife with fraud and abuse. Estimates suggest that 10-15% of all welfare spending is lost to fraud, whether through false claims, identity theft, or other forms of deception. That amounts to $290 billion in taxpayer money—enough to fund critical infrastructure projects or reduce the tax burden on working families. Yet, rather than addressing this systemic failure, the government's answer is always more taxes, more spending, and more oversight. But oversight doesn't fix a broken system—it just adds another layer of bureaucracy to an already bloated machine.

One of the most destructive aspects of the welfare state is its impact on human motivation. In a system where the state guarantees a minimum standard of living, regardless of effort, the incentive to strive for personal excellence disappears. Why push yourself to achieve more when the government will provide for your basic needs? Why take risks, innovate, or work harder when you can receive a check from the government with no strings attached?

The numbers tell the story. Between 2000 and 2020, the number of people receiving government assistance increased by 40%, even as the economy grew. At the same time, the workforce participation rate remained stagnant, hovering around 63%, with millions of able-bodied adults opting out of the workforce altogether. This is not a failure of the economy—it's a failure of the welfare state. When the rewards of hard work are overshadowed by the security of government aid, people stop working.

This isn't just an economic issue—it's a moral one. The welfare state undermines the virtues of self-reliance, personal responsibility, and ambition. It creates a culture of dependency where people are rewarded for doing nothing while those who work hard are punished through higher taxes. This moral erosion is perhaps the most dangerous consequence of the welfare state, as it breeds a society that no longer values achievement or excellence.

The Numbers Don't Lie
Let's back this up with hard data. In 2023, over 68 million Americans

received some form of government assistance, from food stamps to housing subsidies to Medicaid. That's nearly 20% of the population. Of those, nearly 20 million were able-bodied adults without dependents—a group that, in a truly productive society, should be contributing to the economy rather than relying on the government.

Even more concerning is the growing number of people who remain on welfare for extended periods. According to a 2020 study, nearly 25% of welfare recipients had been receiving benefits for over five years. This is a clear indicator that the welfare state is not providing a temporary safety net but fostering long-term dependency. And as more people rely on government assistance, the demand for even more welfare increases, creating a vicious cycle that is nearly impossible to break.

The welfare state doesn't just weaken personal responsibility and productivity—it fosters a culture of envy. It creates an entitled population that believes they deserve what others have earned, without understanding the sacrifice and hard work it takes to achieve success. As the divide between those who work and those who take grows wider, so too does the resentment. This is where envy takes root, breeding the toxic entitlement that's tearing the very fabric of our society.

8

Emulating Failure

The history of the 20th century is marked by the rise and fall of two of the most significant socialist experiments: the Soviet Union under the leadership of Lenin and Stalin, and Maoist China. Both regimes sought to radically transform their societies through the implementation of Marxist-Leninist ideology, but their policies led to catastrophic failures that devastated their populations and left a lasting impact on the world. As the West grapples with its own ideological challenges today, it is crucial to examine the lessons of these historical failures and understand how similar patterns may be emerging in Western societies.

I. The Historical Failures of Soviet Policies:

The Soviet Union, established after the Bolshevik Revolution of 1917, aimed to create a classless, stateless society based on the principles of Marxism-Leninism. However, the implementation of these ideas led to a series of catastrophic policies that resulted in widespread suffering and the eventual collapse of the Soviet state.

Central Planning and Economic Stagnation:

One of the key pillars of Soviet policy was central economic planning. The state controlled all aspects of the economy, from production and distribution to pricing and wages. While this approach initially led to rapid industrialization, it soon became clear that central planning was inherently inefficient. The lack of market signals, such as prices and competition, led to widespread resource misallocation, chronic short-ages of goods, and an overall decline in productivity. By the 1980s, the Soviet economy was in deep crisis, unable to provide for the basic needs of its population or compete with the dynamic economies of the West.

Suppression of Dissent and Human Rights Abuses:

The Soviet regime maintained its grip on power through the ruthless suppression of dissent. Political opponents, intellectuals, and ordinary citizens who expressed any form of opposition were subjected to impris-onment, torture, and execution. The infamous Gulag system of labor camps claimed millions of lives, and the state's surveillance apparatus created an atmosphere of fear and mistrust. The suppression of free speech, independent thought, and political pluralism stifled innovation and led to a stagnant, oppressive society where conformity was enforced at the expense of progress.

The Great Terror and Purges:

Under Stalin's rule, the Soviet Union experienced a period of intense political repression known as the Great Terror. Between 1936 and 1938, millions of people were purged from the Communist Party, the military, and society at large. These purges were characterized by show trials, forced confessions, and widespread executions. The purges decimated the Soviet leadership, creating a culture of paranoia and weakening the state's ability to govern effectively. The terror also had a chilling effect on Soviet society, as individuals were forced to conform or face severe con-sequences.

Agricultural Policies and Famine:

The Soviet Union's collectivization of agriculture, initiated under Stalin, aimed to consolidate individual farms into large, state-controlled collectives. This policy was implemented with brutal force, leading to the displacement of millions of peasants and the destruction of tradi-tional farming practices. The result was widespread famine, most no-tably the Holodomor in Ukraine, where millions of people starved to death. The state's rigid control over agriculture led to persistent food shortages and a decline in agricultural productivity, contributing to the overall failure of the Soviet economy.

II. The Historical Failures of Maoist Policies

Mao Zedong's leadership of China from the founding of the People's Republic in 1949 until his death in 1976 was marked by similarly disastrous policies that mirrored those of the Soviet Union. Maoist ideology sought to create a classless society through radical social and economic transformation, but the implementation of these policies led to immense human suffering and long-term damage to Chinese society.

The Great Leap Forward and Famine:

In 1958, Mao launched the Great Leap Forward, a campaign aimed at rapidly industrializing China and collectivizing agriculture. The policy mandated the creation of large communes and set unrealistic production targets for steel and grain. The Great Leap Forward was a catastrophic failure, resulting in one of the deadliest famines in human history. It is estimated that between 15 and 45 million people died as a result of famine and state violence during this period. The failure of the Great Leap Forward demonstrated the dangers of utopian economic planning and the devastating consequences of ignoring practical realities in pursuit of ideological goals.

The Cultural Revolution and Destruction of Intellectual Life:

The Cultural Revolution, launched by Mao in 1966, aimed to purge Chinese society of bourgeois elements and enforce strict adherence to communist ideology. The movement led to the persecution of intellectuals, artists, and perceived "enemies of the revolution." Universities were closed, books were burned, and cultural heritage was destroyed. The Red Guards, radicalized youth mobilized by Mao, terrorized the population, leading to widespread violence and chaos. The Cultural Revolution decimated China's intellectual and cultural life, setting the country back decades and leaving deep scars on Chinese society.

Political Repression and Human Rights Abuses:

Like the Soviet Union, Maoist China was characterized by severe political repression. The Chinese Communist Party maintained absolute control over the state, and any form of dissent was met with brutal punishment. The state-controlled media and education system were used to indoctrinate the population, suppressing independent thought and enforcing ideological conformity. The legacy of Maoist repression continues to shape China's political system, where dissent is still met with harsh consequences.

III. Introduction to Yuri Bezmenov's Warnings About Ideological Subversion in the West

Yuri Bezmenov, a former KGB agent who defected to the West in the 1970s, provided a chilling warning about the ideological subversion tactics employed by the Soviet Union to undermine Western societies. Bezmenov's insights are particularly relevant today, as the West faces internal challenges that echo the ideological strategies he described.

The Four Stages of Ideological Subversion:

Bezmenov outlined a four-stage process of ideological subversion used by the Soviet Union to weaken and destabilize target nations:

Demoralization: The first stage involves a sustained campaign to undermine the moral and ideological foundations of a society. This is achieved by promoting relativism, undermining traditional values, and fostering a sense of apathy and cynicism. The goal is to erode the confidence of individuals in their own culture and institutions.

Destabilization: In the second stage, the subverted society experiences growing instability in its political, economic, and social systems. This is often accompanied by the polarization of society, the weakening of public trust in institutions, and the rise of extremist movements.

Crisis: The third stage is marked by a significant crisis, whether political, economic, or social, that threatens the stability of the nation. This crisis creates an opportunity for external or internal actors to seize power or impose radical changes.

Normalization: The final stage occurs when the new order is established, often under the guise of restoring stability. This stage solidifies the changes made during the crisis, leading to the entrenchment of new power structures and ideologies.

Demoralization in the West:

According to Bezmenov, the West has been subjected to a prolonged period of demoralization, particularly through the influence of Marxist-Leninist ideas in education, media, and culture. He argued that this demoralization has led to a weakening of Western values, such as individualism, personal responsibility, and meritocracy, and has paved the way for the rise of identity politics, relativism, and anti-capitalist sentiments.

The Relevance of Bezmenov's Warnings Today:

Many of Bezmenov's predictions appear to be coming to fruition in the contemporary West. The polarization of politics, the erosion of trust in institutions, and the rise of movements that challenge the foundations of Western society are all indicative of the destabilization stage he described. The increasing influence of ideologies that reject the principles of free markets, individual rights, and limited government further suggests that the West may be moving toward a crisis point.

The Soviet Experience: Lessons from Central Planning, Suppression of Dissent, and the Erosion of Individual Responsibility

The Soviet Union, founded on Marxist-Leninist principles, sought to create a utopian society through the implementation of radical economic, political, and social policies. However, these policies—central planning, suppression of dissent, and the erosion of individual responsibility—proved disastrous for the Soviet state. They stifled competence, innovation, and societal well-being, leading to the eventual collapse of the Soviet Union. Today, the West faces its own challenges, with trends in governance, education, and culture that bear concerning similarities to those that led to the Soviet Union's downfall.

I. Analysis of Soviet Policies: Central Planning, Suppression of Dissent, and the Erosion of Individual Responsibility

Central Planning:

Economic Centralization: The Soviet economy was based on the principle of central planning, where the state controlled all aspects of economic life, from production quotas to pricing and distribution. The government created five-year plans that dictated the allocation of resources, the types of goods to be produced, and the targets for industrial output.

Lack of Market Mechanisms: Without the price signals and competition inherent in market economies, central planning led to widespread inefficiency. Resources were often misallocated, leading to chronic shortages of basic goods, such as food and consumer products, while overproduction occurred in sectors deemed important by the state, such as heavy industry and military hardware.

Stifling of Innovation: Central planning left little room for innovation or entrepreneurship. The focus on meeting quotas and adhering to rigid state directives discouraged risk-taking and creative problem-solving. The absence of incentives for individuals and businesses to innovate led to technological stagnation and an inability to compete with more dynamic, market-driven economies in the West.

Suppression of Dissent:

Political Repression: The Soviet regime maintained its power through the systematic suppression of dissent. Political opponents, intellectuals, and ordinary citizens who expressed criticism of the state were subjected to surveillance, arrest, imprisonment, and even execution. The fear of repression created a culture of conformity, where expressing independent thought or challenging the state's authority was dangerous.

Censorship and Propaganda: The Soviet government tightly controlled the flow of information, using state media to propagate its ideology and censoring any content that contradicted the official narrative. Schools and universities were also instruments of state control, where curricula were designed to indoctrinate students in Marxist-Leninist ideology and discourage critical thinking.

The Effect on Civil Society: The suppression of dissent extended beyond politics into every aspect of life. Civic organizations, religious groups, and any form of social organization that was not under state control were either co-opted or destroyed. This left individuals isolated, unable to organize or advocate for their rights, and deeply dependent on the state for their livelihoods.

Erosion of Individual Responsibility:

Collectivism Over Individualism: The Soviet state promoted collectivism as a core value, subordinating individual needs and desires to the supposed greater good of the state. Personal initiative was discouraged, and individuals were expected to conform to the collective will as determined by the Communist Party.

Dependence on the State: The erosion of individual responsibility was most evident in the widespread dependence on the state for all aspects of life, from employment to housing and healthcare. The promise of cradle-to-grave security, while appealing in theory, led to a loss of personal agency and a culture of passivity. Citizens were taught to rely on the state rather than take responsibility for their own success or failure.

Moral and Ethical Decline: The suppression of religion, traditional values, and independent moral frameworks further contributed to the erosion of individual responsibility. Without a guiding moral compass outside the state's ideology, individuals lacked the ethical foundations to resist corruption, dishonesty, and the pursuit of self-interest at the expense of the collective.

II. The Impact of These Policies on Competence, Innovation, and Societal Well-Being

Competence:

Diminished Work Ethic: The Soviet system, by eliminating competition and merit-based rewards, led to a decline in work ethic and overall competence. With no incentive to excel or innovate, workers became complacent, and productivity suffered. The lack of accountability and the focus on meeting state-mandated quotas rather than producing quality goods further undermined competence across all sectors of the economy.

Brain Drain: The suppression of intellectual freedom and the state's control over education and research drove many of the Soviet Union's brightest minds to seek opportunities abroad or to withdraw from meaningful participation in society. This brain drain, coupled with the state's discouragement of independent thought, led to a severe decline in scientific and technological advancement.

Innovation:

Stagnation of Technological Progress: The central planning model stifled innovation by focusing on short-term production goals rather than long-term development. Without the competition and incentives that drive innovation in market economies, the Soviet Union fell behind technologically. While the state did achieve some successes in specific areas, such as space exploration, these were exceptions rather than the rule, and were often achieved at great human and economic cost.

Lack of Entrepreneurial Spirit: The suppression of private enterprise and the emphasis on state control meant that entrepreneurial activity was virtually non-existent in the Soviet Union. The absence of small businesses and private innovation not only limited economic diversity but also stifled the development of new industries and technologies that could have driven growth.

Societal Well-Being:

Widespread Poverty: The inefficiencies of the centrally planned economy, combined with the state's prioritization of military and industrial production over consumer goods, led to widespread poverty and deprivation. Basic necessities were often scarce, and the quality of life for most Soviet citizens was far below that of their counterparts in the West.

Psychological and Social Impact: The constant surveillance, repression, and lack of personal freedom took a heavy toll on the psychological well-being of the Soviet population. Fear, distrust, and a sense of hopelessness permeated society, leading to widespread apathy, alcoholism, and other social ills. The breakdown of family structures and traditional values further contributed to a decline in societal well-being.

III. Comparison with Current Trends in Western Governance, Education, and Culture

Central Planning in the West:

Growing Government Intervention: In recent years, there has been a trend in the West towards greater government intervention in the economy, with increasing regulation, centralization, and control over various sectors. While this is not the same as Soviet-style central planning, the move towards more state involvement in areas such as healthcare, energy, and finance raises concerns about the potential for inefficiency, misallocation of resources, and a decline in innovation.

Economic Centralization and Technocracy: The rise of technocratic governance, where decisions are made by experts rather than elected representatives, mirrors the Soviet emphasis on central planning by elites. While technocracy can bring efficiency, it can also lead to a disconnect between decision-makers and the needs and desires of the broader population, reducing accountability and stifling grassroots innovation.

Suppression of Dissent in the West:

Censorship and Cancel Culture: The increasing prevalence of censorship, whether through government policies, social media platforms, or cultural norms, is a troubling trend in the West. The rise of "cancel culture," where individuals and ideas are silenced or ostracized for deviating from prevailing orthodoxy, echoes the Soviet suppression of dissent. This environment discourages open debate, critical thinking, and intellectual diversity, which are essential for a healthy, innovative society.

Ideological Conformity in Education: In Western educational institutions, there is growing concern about the promotion of ideological conformity, where certain viewpoints are privileged while others are marginalized or excluded. This trend undermines academic freedom and the pursuit of knowledge, leading to an environment where students are discouraged from questioning or challenging established ideas—parallels to the indoctrination practices in Soviet education.

Erosion of Individual Responsibility in the West:

Dependence on the State: The expansion of welfare programs and the increasing role of the state in providing for citizens' needs have led to a culture of dependence in some segments of Western society. While social safety nets are essential, there is a risk that over-reliance on the state can erode individual responsibility, initiative, and the work ethic that drives economic and social progress.

Collectivism and Identity Politics: The rise of identity politics in the West, where individuals are increasingly defined by their group identity rather than their personal achievements or character, mirrors the collectivist ideology of the Soviet Union. This trend undermines the principles of individualism and meritocracy, leading to social fragmentation and a decline in personal responsibility.

Maoist China: Cultural Revolution and Its Aftermath

The Cultural Revolution, one of the most tumultuous periods in modern Chinese history, was a decade-long political movement launched by Mao Zedong in 1966. It aimed to reassert Mao's control over the Communist Party and to radically transform Chinese society by purging it of "bourgeois" elements, capitalist influences, and perceived enemies of the revolution. The Cultural Revolution had catastrophic effects on Chinese society, leading to widespread violence, the destruction of cultural heritage, the suppression of intellectualism, and the erosion of meritocracy. As we examine this dark chapter in history, it is important to consider the parallels between Maoist policies and current trends in the West that similarly challenge free speech, historical narratives, and academic freedom.

I. Overview of the Cultural Revolution and Its Catastrophic Effects on Chinese Society

The Origins and Goals of the Cultural Revolution:

The Cultural Revolution was initiated by Mao Zedong, who feared that the Communist Party was becoming too bureaucratic and that capitalist elements were infiltrating Chinese society. To combat this perceived threat, Mao called on China's youth to rise up and purge the country of these elements, leading to the formation of the Red Guards, a radicalized youth movement.

The stated goals of the Cultural Revolution were to preserve and enforce communist ideology by removing traditional, capitalist, and cultural elements from Chinese society. Mao sought to create a classless society in which loyalty to the Communist Party and its ideology was paramount.

The Purge of "Enemies of the Revolution":

The Cultural Revolution quickly devolved into a campaign of terror, as the Red Guards and other revolutionary groups targeted intellectuals, party officials, teachers, and ordinary citizens who were deemed to be enemies of the revolution. These individuals were subjected to public humiliation, beatings, imprisonment, and execution. The movement encouraged widespread denunciations, where even neighbors and family members turned on each other in a climate of fear and suspicion.

The Cultural Revolution also targeted China's traditional culture, including its Confucian heritage, religious institutions, and ancient cultural practices. Temples, artworks, and historical artifacts were destroyed, and scholars of traditional culture were persecuted. The Red Guards sought to erase any remnants of China's pre-communist past in their quest to build a new revolutionary society.

Societal Breakdown and Economic Disruption:

The Cultural Revolution led to the near-total collapse of China's educational system, as schools and universities were closed, teachers were persecuted, and the curriculum was replaced with revolutionary propaganda. The economy also suffered, as industries were disrupted by the chaotic political climate, and agricultural production plummeted due to the upheaval in rural areas.

The destruction of social structures and the suppression of intellectual and cultural life resulted in a generation of Chinese youth who were deprived of a formal education and deeply traumatized by the violence and chaos of the period. The long-term social and psychological effects of the Cultural Revolution were profound, leaving scars that would affect Chinese society for decades.

II. The Destruction of Cultural Heritage, Intellectualism, and the Erosion of Meritocracy

Destruction of Cultural Heritage:

The Cultural Revolution's assault on China's cultural heritage was one of its most devastating aspects. The Red Guards were encouraged to destroy anything associated with the "Four Olds": old customs, old culture, old habits, and old ideas. This campaign led to the widespread destruction of temples, historical sites, and cultural artifacts, as well as the burning of books and the suppression of traditional arts and practices.

The cultural annihilation aimed to sever China's connection with its past and replace it with a new, revolutionary culture based solely on Maoist ideology. This loss of cultural heritage not only robbed China of its rich history but also contributed to a sense of dislocation and identity crisis among its people.

Suppression of Intellectualism:

Intellectuals were among the primary targets of the Cultural Revolution. Academics, writers, and scientists were labeled as "bourgeois" and "counter-revolutionary" and were subjected to public humiliation, forced labor, and re-education campaigns. Universities were closed, and academic freedom was entirely suppressed as the focus shifted to ideological indoctrination.

The persecution of intellectuals led to a significant brain drain, as those who survived the initial purges were often sent to the countryside for manual labor, effectively removing them from intellectual and cultural life. This decimation of the intellectual class stifled innovation, scientific progress, and cultural development, leaving China intellectually impoverished.

Erosion of Meritocracy:

The Cultural Revolution also eroded the concept of meritocracy in China. Success and advancement within society and the Communist Party became increasingly dependent on one's loyalty to Mao and adherence to revolutionary ideology rather than on competence, education, or achievement. This shift led to the promotion of unqualified individuals who were fervently loyal to Mao but lacked the skills and knowledge needed to govern effectively or contribute to society.

The prioritization of ideological purity over merit had long-lasting effects on Chinese society, undermining trust in institutions and creating a culture of sycophancy and corruption. The erosion of meritocracy contributed to the overall decline in societal well-being and economic productivity during the Cultural Revolution.

III. Parallels Between Maoist Policies and Current Western Movements
  Challenges to Free Speech:

In Maoist China, free speech was severely curtailed, with any deviation from the official party line met with harsh punishment. Today, similar patterns are emerging in the West, where certain viewpoints are increasingly censored or silenced through social and institutional pressure. The rise of "cancel culture" and the policing of speech in academia, media, and public discourse echo the suppression of dissent seen during the Cultural Revolution.

In both contexts, the suppression of free speech is justified by the need to protect ideological purity and prevent the spread of "harmful" ideas. However, this approach stifles open debate, critical thinking, and the diversity of thought that are essential for a healthy, democratic society.

Rewriting Historical Narratives:

The Cultural Revolution sought to erase and rewrite China's history to align with Maoist ideology, often through the destruction of cultural artifacts and the revision of historical narratives. In the West, there are growing movements that challenge and seek to revise historical narratives, often with the goal of addressing historical injustices. While these efforts can bring important perspectives to light, they can also lead to the oversimplification or distortion of history.

The danger lies in the potential for these movements to become dogmatic, where only one interpretation of history is allowed, and dissenting views are marginalized or suppressed. This approach risks creating a sanitized or one-dimensional view of history, much like the version of history promoted during the Cultural Revolution.

Threats to Academic Freedom:

During the Cultural Revolution, academic freedom was entirely subordinated to political ideology, with education becoming a tool for indoctrination rather than a means of pursuing knowledge. In the West, there are increasing concerns that academic institutions are becoming ideological battlegrounds, where certain ideas and perspectives are privileged while others are excluded.

The growing trend of "de-platforming" speakers, the imposition of ideological litmus tests in hiring and curriculum design, and the pressure on academics to conform to prevailing ideological trends all mirror the ways in which intellectual freedom was curtailed in Maoist China. These trends threaten the integrity of education and the pursuit of truth, leading to an environment where critical inquiry is stifled.

9

Case Studies

Detroit: The Fall of an Industrial Giant—
A Detailed Analysis of Decline Due to Incompetence, Corruption, and the Abandonment of Meritocracy

Detroit, once hailed as the "Arsenal of Democracy" and the epicenter of America's industrial might, now stands as a stark symbol of urban decay and economic collapse. The city's rise to prominence in the early 20th century, driven by the booming automobile industry, made it one of the wealthiest and most innovative cities in the world. However, by the latter half of the century, Detroit's fortunes had dramatically reversed, leading to widespread poverty, crime, and abandonment. The decline of this industrial giant can be traced to a combination of incompetence, corruption, and the abandonment of meritocracy, all of which conspired to bring down a city that was once synonymous with American success.

The Rise of Detroit: A Beacon of American Industry

Detroit's ascent began in the late 19th and early 20th centuries, as it became the hub of America's burgeoning automobile industry. Pioneers like Henry Ford, the Dodge brothers, and Walter Chrysler established manufacturing plants in the city, turning Detroit into the epicenter of automotive innovation. The introduction of assembly line production by Ford revolutionized manufacturing, making cars affordable for the average American and cementing Detroit's status as the Motor City.

The city thrived on the back of this industrial boom. By the 1940s and 1950s, Detroit had become one of the most prosperous cities in the United States. The automobile industry provided well-paying jobs, fueling a robust middle class and creating a vibrant urban environment. Detroit's population swelled to nearly 2 million people, and the city was renowned for its cultural offerings, impressive architecture, and thriving communities. It was a place where hard work and innovation were rewarded, and where the American Dream seemed within reach for all.

The seeds of Detroit's decline were sown in the post-World War II era, as a combination of economic, social, and political challenges began to undermine the city's stability. One of the primary economic factors was the increasing competition from foreign automakers, particularly from Japan and Germany. These companies produced cars that were more fuel-efficient and reliable than their American counterparts, leading to a decline in the market share of Detroit's Big Three automakers: Ford, General Motors, and Chrysler.

The oil crises of the 1970s exacerbated these challenges, as American consumers turned to smaller, more fuel-efficient vehicles produced by foreign manufacturers. Detroit's automakers, burdened by large, inefficient production methods and a bloated workforce, struggled to adapt to these changing market conditions. The result was a significant decline in the profitability of the automobile industry, leading to plant closures, layoffs, and a shrinking tax base for the city.

Social factors also played a critical role in Detroit's decline. The city experienced significant racial tensions throughout the 20th century, culminating in the 1967 Detroit riot, one of the most destructive urban uprisings in American history. The riot was a response to long-standing issues of racial inequality, police brutality, and economic disparity. The aftermath of the riot saw a mass exodus of white residents and businesses to the suburbs, a phenomenon known as "white flight." This demographic shift further eroded the city's tax base and left behind a predominantly African American population that struggled with poverty and unemployment.

Incompetence and Corruption: The Betrayal of Public Trust

As Detroit's economic and social challenges mounted, the city increasingly fell victim to incompetence and corruption within its political leadership. The decline of meritocracy in city governance and public institutions played a significant role in accelerating Detroit's downfall.

Political incompetence in Detroit was characterized by short-sighted policies, poor fiscal management, and an inability to adapt to changing economic realities. The city government, faced with a declining tax base, responded by increasing taxes on the remaining businesses and residents, further driving people and companies out of the city. Rather than implementing structural reforms to address the underlying economic issues, city officials often opted for temporary fixes that exacerbated the long-term problems.

Corruption became rampant in Detroit's government, eroding public trust and further weakening the city's ability to respond to its challenges. One of the most notorious examples of corruption was the administration of Mayor Kwame Kilpatrick, who served from 2002 to 2008. Kilpatrick's tenure was marked by a series of scandals, including charges of perjury, obstruction of justice, and misuse of public funds. Kilpatrick's administration was emblematic of a broader culture of corruption that plagued Detroit's government for decades, where public officials prioritized personal gain over the welfare of the city and its residents.

The abandonment of meritocracy in city governance and public institutions compounded these issues. Political appointments and public sector jobs increasingly became based on cronyism and patronage rather than competence and merit. This led to a decline in the effectiveness of public services, from education to law enforcement, and contributed to the overall deterioration of the city's infrastructure and social fabric.

The lack of qualified and motivated leadership at all levels of government created a situation where the city's problems were allowed to fester and grow, ultimately leading to the collapse of Detroit's municipal government in 2013 when the city filed for the largest municipal bankruptcy in U.S. history.

The decline of Detroit's automobile industry was both a cause and a consequence of the city's broader economic and social collapse. As the Big Three automakers struggled to compete with foreign manufacturers, they began to close plants and lay off workers in Detroit. The city's industrial base, which had been the engine of its prosperity, steadily eroded, leading to widespread unemployment and poverty.

The collapse of the automobile industry had a cascading effect on the city's economy. Businesses that depended on the auto industry—suppliers, parts manufacturers, and service providers—also suffered, leading to further job losses and economic decline. As the city's industrial base crumbled, so too did its commercial and residential areas. Once-thriving neighborhoods became ghost towns, with abandoned buildings and vacant lots replacing bustling streets and vibrant communities.

The decline of the auto industry also had significant implications for Detroit's physical infrastructure. The city's roads, bridges, and public transportation systems, which had been built to support a large industrial workforce, fell into disrepair as the tax base dwindled. The failure to maintain and upgrade infrastructure further discouraged investment and development, creating a vicious cycle of decline.

The Human Cost: Poverty, Crime, and Social Decay

The human cost of Detroit's decline has been immense. As the city's economy collapsed, so too did the quality of life for its residents. Poverty rates soared, with nearly 40% of Detroit's population living below the poverty line by the early 21st century. Unemployment became endemic, particularly among the city's African American population, leading to a sense of hopelessness and despair.

The decline in economic opportunities was accompanied by a sharp rise in crime. Detroit, once known for its vibrant cultural scene and thriving communities, became infamous for its high rates of violent crime. The city's police force, weakened by budget cuts and plagued by corruption, struggled to maintain order, leading to a breakdown in public safety. The high crime rates further discouraged investment and drove more residents out of the city, deepening the cycle of decline.

Education, another pillar of the city's future, also suffered. Detroit's public school system, once a source of pride, became one of the worst in the nation. Underfunded, overcrowded, and mismanaged, the schools failed to provide students with the education and skills needed to escape the cycle of poverty. The lack of educational opportunities further contributed to the decline of the city's workforce and the erosion of social mobility.

Detroit's fall from grace offers a powerful lesson about the importance of competence, integrity, and meritocracy in governance and industry. The city's decline was not inevitable; it was the result of a series of failures—economic, social, and political—that could have been addressed with strong, visionary leadership. Instead, incompetence, corruption, and the abandonment of meritocracy allowed these problems to fester and grow, ultimately leading to the collapse of one of America's greatest cities.

The story of Detroit underscores the dangers of allowing short-term thinking, political cronyism, and a culture of entitlement to undermine the principles of meritocracy. When public officials are selected based on loyalty rather than competence, when decisions are made for political gain rather than the public good, and when success is punished rather than rewarded, the result is a society that is unable to adapt to challenges or seize opportunities.

Moreover, Detroit's decline illustrates the interconnectedness of economic, social, and political factors. The failure of the auto industry, the exodus of businesses and residents, and the collapse of public institutions were not isolated events; they were the result of systemic failures that reinforced each other. Addressing these issues required a holistic approach that Detroit's leaders were unable—or unwilling—to provide.

The European Welfare State: Dependency and Decay—How Welfare Dependency Has Stifled Innovation and Led to Economic and Social Stagnation

The European welfare state, once celebrated as a model of social security and economic equality, is increasingly viewed as a double-edged sword. While it has undeniably provided a safety net for millions of citizens, ensuring access to healthcare, education, and income support, it has also fostered a culture of dependency that has stifled innovation, reduced economic dynamism, and led to social stagnation. This system, designed to protect the vulnerable, has inadvertently created a cycle of dependency that discourages self-reliance, undermines the work ethic, and hampers the ability of European nations to compete in a rapidly changing global economy.

The Origins and Expansion of the European Welfare State

The modern European welfare state emerged in the aftermath of World War II, as European nations sought to rebuild their economies and ensure social stability. The horrors of the war, combined with the Great Depression that preceded it, led to widespread support for a new social contract that would protect citizens from the extremes of poverty, unemployment, and ill health. This social contract was based on the principles of universal social insurance, state-sponsored healthcare, free education, and income support for those in need.

In the decades that followed, the welfare state expanded significantly, fueled by the post-war economic boom and the rise of social democratic governments across Europe. The guiding philosophy behind the welfare state was that the government had a responsibility to provide for the basic needs of all citizens, thereby reducing inequality and ensuring that everyone had the opportunity to lead a decent life. This philosophy was enshrined in a wide range of social programs, from unemployment benefits and pensions to housing assistance and child care subsidies.

For many years, the welfare state was credited with helping to create the prosperous, stable societies that characterized much of Western Europe. By providing a safety net for the most vulnerable, the welfare state helped to reduce poverty, promote social cohesion, and ensure a relatively high standard of living for the majority of citizens. However, as the welfare state grew, so too did its costs and the unintended consequences that came with it.

One of the most significant unintended consequences of the European welfare state has been the rise of welfare dependency. What began as a safety net for those in need has, in many cases, become a trap that discourages work, innovation, and self-reliance. The extensive benefits provided by the welfare state—while well-intentioned—have created perverse incentives that have led to a growing number of individuals and families relying on government assistance as a way of life, rather than as a temporary support during difficult times.

Welfare dependency has been exacerbated by the structure of many welfare programs, which often penalize work or entrepreneurship. For example, in some countries, the loss of benefits due to earning income from work can be so steep that it creates what economists call a "poverty trap," where individuals are better off remaining unemployed or underemployed than taking on full-time work. This disincentive to work not only undermines individual initiative but also reduces the overall labor force participation rate, leading to lower productivity and economic growth.

The culture of dependency fostered by the welfare state has also had a significant impact on innovation and entrepreneurship. In societies where a significant portion of the population relies on government assistance, the drive to take risks, start businesses, or pursue new ideas is often diminished. The guaranteed security provided by the welfare state can lead to complacency, where individuals prioritize the stability of state support over the uncertainties and potential rewards of entrepreneurial activity. This stifling of innovation has long-term consequences for economic dynamism, as the creation of new businesses and industries is essential for sustained economic growth and job creation.

Economic Stagnation and the Burden of the Welfare State

The economic consequences of welfare dependency are particularly evident in the stagnation experienced by many European economies. The generous social benefits provided by the welfare state are funded through high taxes on both individuals and businesses, which can dampen economic activity. High taxes reduce disposable income, discourage investment, and create a drag on economic growth. In addition, the large public sector required to administer and sustain the welfare state often leads to inefficiencies and bureaucratic inertia, further stifling innovation and economic dynamism.

The burden of the welfare state is particularly pronounced in countries with aging populations, where the costs of pensions, healthcare, and elder care are rising rapidly. As the ratio of working-age individuals to retirees declines, the financial sustainability of the welfare state comes into question. Governments are forced to either raise taxes, cut benefits, or borrow heavily to meet their obligations, all of which have negative consequences for economic growth and social stability.

The economic stagnation resulting from the welfare state is also reflected in the high levels of youth unemployment seen in many European countries. In nations like Spain, Italy, and Greece, youth unemployment rates have remained stubbornly high, even as overall economic conditions have improved. This is partly due to the rigidity of labor markets, which are often characterized by strong protections for older workers and high barriers to entry for younger workers. The welfare state, while providing income support for the unemployed, does little to address the underlying structural issues that prevent young people from entering the workforce and gaining the experience necessary for long-term employment.

Moreover, the reliance on welfare benefits has led to a decline in social mobility. In a society where many people are dependent on government assistance, the opportunities for upward mobility are limited. The welfare state, by providing a baseline level of income and services, can inadvertently create a sense of complacency, where individuals are less motivated to pursue higher education, better jobs, or entrepreneurial ventures. This lack of ambition and drive contributes to the economic stagnation seen in many parts of Europe, where the gap between the wealthy and the rest of the population continues to widen.

The social consequences of welfare dependency are equally concerning. The culture of dependency fostered by the welfare state has led to the erosion of traditional community and family structures, which have historically played a crucial role in providing support and fostering social cohesion. In many cases, the welfare state has replaced these structures, leading to a decline in personal responsibility and community engagement.

The reliance on government assistance has also contributed to the fragmentation of society, as individuals become more isolated and less connected to their communities. The sense of entitlement that often accompanies welfare dependency can lead to a breakdown in social trust, as people come to view government support as a right rather than a temporary help. This mentality undermines the social fabric, as individuals are less likely to contribute to their communities, volunteer, or help others in need.

The welfare state has also had a significant impact on the family unit. In some cases, welfare programs have created disincentives for marriage and family formation, particularly when benefits are structured in such a way that single-parent households receive more support than two-parent households. This has contributed to the decline of the traditional family structure in many parts of Europe, with long-term consequences for social stability and child well-being.

The erosion of community and family structures, coupled with the rise of welfare dependency, has led to a sense of social stagnation in many European countries. The decline in social mobility, the fragmentation of communities, and the weakening of family bonds have all contributed to a sense of hopelessness and disillusionment among large segments of the population. This social stagnation is reflected in the rise of populist movements across Europe, as disaffected citizens seek to challenge the status quo and express their frustration with the lack of opportunities for upward mobility and self-improvement.

The European welfare state is at a crossroads. While it has undoubtedly provided a safety net for millions of citizens and helped to reduce poverty and inequality, it has also created a culture of dependency that stifles innovation, reduces economic dynamism, and leads to social stagnation. The challenge for European governments is to reform the welfare state in a way that preserves its core principles of social protection and equality while addressing the unintended consequences that have led to dependency and decay.

Reforming the welfare state will require a shift in focus from providing passive income support to promoting active participation in the labor market and society. This could include measures such as reducing the disincentives to work and entrepreneurship, reforming labor market regulations to make it easier for young people to enter the workforce, and investing in education and training programs that equip individuals with the skills they need to succeed in a rapidly changing economy.

In addition to economic reforms, there must be a renewed emphasis on personal responsibility, community engagement, and social cohesion. Governments, civil society, and the private sector all have a role to play in fostering a culture of self-reliance and personal initiative, where individuals are encouraged to take responsibility for their own lives and contribute to the well-being of their communities. This will require a rethinking of the role of the welfare state, from one that simply provides benefits to one that empowers individuals to achieve their full potential.

Finally, the sustainability of the welfare state will depend on addressing the demographic challenges facing Europe. As the population ages, governments will need to find ways to reduce the burden on the working-age population while ensuring that the needs of the elderly are met. This could include measures such as raising the retirement age, encouraging greater labor force participation among older workers, and promoting policies that support family formation and population growth.

The American Education System: A Case Study on How It Has Become a Breeding Ground for Entitlement Rather Than Competence

The American education system, once heralded as a beacon of opportunity and a key driver of social mobility, is now facing widespread criticism for fostering a culture of entitlement rather than one of competence and achievement. Over the past several decades, a combination of misguided policies, shifting cultural values, and a focus on inclusivity over excellence has transformed schools and universities into environments where the pursuit of knowledge and skill development has taken a backseat to the cultivation of self-esteem and entitlement. This case study examines the factors that have contributed to this shift and the consequences it has had for both individual students and the broader society.

The American education system was originally built on the principles of meritocracy and the belief that hard work, discipline, and intellectual curiosity were the keys to success. From the early days of the republic, education was seen as a critical component of the American Dream—a means by which individuals from all backgrounds could rise through the ranks of society based on their abilities and efforts. Public schools, land-grant universities, and the proliferation of community colleges were all designed to provide opportunities for students to develop the skills and knowledge necessary to succeed in a rapidly industrializing nation.

Throughout much of the 20th century, the American education system was a model of excellence, producing world-class scientists, engineers, and thinkers who helped drive innovation and economic growth. However, beginning in the latter half of the 20th century, a series of cultural and policy shifts began to erode the meritocratic foundations of the system, leading to the rise of a culture of entitlement.

One of the most significant factors contributing to the rise of entitlement in the American education system has been the shift in educational priorities from academic achievement to the cultivation of self-esteem. This shift began in the 1960s and 1970s, as educators and policymakers became increasingly concerned with issues of equity and inclusivity. The emphasis on ensuring that all students felt valued and included led to the adoption of policies and practices that prioritized self-esteem over academic rigor.

One of the most visible manifestations of this shift has been the widespread practice of grade inflation. In an effort to avoid discouraging students or damaging their self-esteem, many schools began to lower academic standards and inflate grades. This practice has become so pervasive that a "B" grade, which once signified above-average performance, is now often considered average or even below average in many institutions. As a result, students are frequently rewarded with high grades regardless of their actual performance or understanding of the material.

Another consequence of this shift has been the de-emphasis of competition and merit-based achievement. Many schools have moved away from traditional practices such as class rankings, valedictorian honors, and academic awards, arguing that these practices create unnecessary pressure and contribute to inequality. Instead, schools have adopted a more egalitarian approach, where participation and effort are often rewarded as much, if not more, than actual achievement. This has led to a culture where students come to expect recognition and rewards regardless of their performance, fostering a sense of entitlement that undermines the values of hard work and excellence.

The federal government's involvement in education, particularly through the No Child Left Behind Act (NCLB) of 2001, has also played a significant role in the rise of entitlement in the American education system. While NCLB was intended to raise academic standards and hold schools accountable for student performance, its emphasis on standardized testing and meeting minimum proficiency levels has had the unintended consequence of lowering academic expectations.

Under NCLB, schools were required to ensure that all students met certain proficiency levels in reading and math, or face penalties. While this policy was designed to close the achievement gap, it often led to a narrowing of the curriculum and a focus on "teaching to the test." Teachers, under pressure to meet federal mandates, were forced to prioritize basic skills and test preparation over deeper, more challenging content. This focus on minimum proficiency levels, rather than on fostering excellence, contributed to a culture where meeting the bare minimum became the primary goal, rather than striving for higher levels of achievement.

Moreover, the focus on standardized testing has led to the standardization of mediocrity. In an effort to ensure that all students meet the required proficiency levels, schools have increasingly adopted a one-size-fits-all approach to education, where the needs of individual students are often secondary to the demands of the testing regime. This has stifled creativity, innovation, and critical thinking, as students are trained to pass tests rather than to engage with complex ideas or pursue their intellectual interests.

The Consequences of Entitlement in Higher Education

The culture of entitlement fostered in K-12 education has had significant repercussions in higher education as well. Colleges and universities, under pressure to attract and retain students, have increasingly adopted policies that cater to students' desires rather than challenging them to meet high academic standards. This has led to the proliferation of "safe spaces," trigger warnings, and policies that prioritize student comfort over intellectual rigor.

One of the most concerning trends in higher education is the decline in academic rigor. In an effort to keep students satisfied and ensure high retention rates, many universities have lowered academic standards, inflated grades, and reduced the workload in courses. This has led to a situation where many students graduate with degrees that hold little value, as they have not been challenged to develop the critical thinking, problem-solving, and communication skills that are essential for success in the real world.

The rise of entitlement in higher education has also contributed to the phenomenon of "credentialism," where the possession of a degree is seen as more important than the knowledge and skills that the degree is supposed to represent. As more students pursue higher education, often with the expectation that a degree will automatically lead to a well-paying job, the value of a college degree has become increasingly diluted. This has led to a situation where many graduates find themselves underemployed or struggling to find work that matches their qualifications, fueling frustration and disillusionment.

The entitlement culture fostered by the American education system has broader implications for society as a whole. One of the most significant consequences is the erosion of the work ethic and the devaluation of personal responsibility. When students are taught to expect rewards without effort and to prioritize self-esteem over achievement, they are less likely to develop the resilience, perseverance, and work ethic needed to succeed in the real world.

This has led to a generation of young people who are often unprepared for the challenges of the workforce. Employers increasingly report that many recent graduates lack the basic skills and work ethic needed to thrive in a competitive environment. This skills gap has significant economic implications, as it reduces productivity, stifles innovation, and limits the ability of the United States to compete in a global economy.

The entitlement mentality also has social consequences, as it contributes to a sense of disillusionment and frustration among young people who find that the rewards they were promised do not materialize in the real world. This has fueled a growing sense of grievance and victimhood, where individuals are more likely to blame external factors for their lack of success rather than taking responsibility for their own lives and actions. This mentality undermines social cohesion and contributes to the polarization and division that are increasingly evident in American society.

Addressing the entitlement culture in the American education system requires a fundamental shift in how education is approached and valued. One of the most important steps is to restore the emphasis on academic rigor and merit-based achievement. Schools and universities must set high standards and challenge students to meet them, rather than lowering expectations to ensure that everyone feels successful. This means reintroducing competition, rewarding excellence, and holding students accountable for their performance.

Educational reform must also focus on developing the skills and attributes that are essential for success in the real world. This includes not only academic knowledge but also critical thinking, problem-solving, communication, and the ability to work collaboratively. Schools should prioritize these skills over rote memorization and test preparation, ensuring that students are prepared to meet the challenges of a rapidly changing world.

In addition, there must be a renewed emphasis on personal responsibility and the work ethic. Students must be taught that success is earned, not given, and that failure is a part of the learning process. This requires a cultural shift away from the focus on self-esteem and toward the development of resilience, perseverance, and the willingness to take risks and learn from mistakes.

Finally, policymakers and educators must work to reduce the focus on standardized testing and the bureaucratization of education. While accountability is important, it must be balanced with the need for flexibility and innovation in the classroom. Teachers should be given the freedom to tailor their instruction to the needs of their students, encouraging creativity, intellectual curiosity, and a love of learning.

10

Reclaiming Competence

H ow Reclaiming the Value of Individual Responsibility Is Key to Reversing the Competency Crisis

Restoring Individual Responsibility: How Reclaiming the Value of Individual Responsibility Is Key to Reversing the Competency Crisis

In the face of a growing competency crisis across the Western world, where mediocrity has supplanted excellence and dependency has overshadowed self-reliance, restoring the value of individual responsibility emerges as a crucial solution. The decline in competence across various sectors—from education to industry—can largely be traced back to a cultural shift away from the values of personal accountability, hard work, and self-determination. Reversing this trend requires a renewed emphasis on individual responsibility as the cornerstone of personal success and societal progress.

The Decline of Individual Responsibility

The erosion of individual responsibility in Western societies is the result of several interrelated factors, including the expansion of the welfare state, the rise of entitlement culture, and the devaluation of meritocracy. Over the past several decades, these factors have converged to create an environment where individuals are increasingly encouraged to look to external sources—whether government, institutions, or others—for support and success, rather than relying on their own efforts and abilities.

The welfare state, while providing necessary safety nets for the most vulnerable, has in many cases contributed to a culture of dependency. When individuals are assured of basic needs without having to work for them, the incentive to strive for self-improvement and to take responsibility for one's own life diminishes. This has led to a situation where large segments of the population are more focused on what they can receive from society rather than what they can contribute.

Entitlement culture has further exacerbated this decline in responsibility. The belief that one is owed certain privileges or outcomes, regardless of effort or merit, undermines the values of hard work and perseverance. When individuals are taught to expect success without sacrifice, they are less likely to develop the resilience and determination necessary to overcome challenges and achieve long-term goals.

The devaluation of meritocracy, where success is increasingly decoupled from competence and effort, has also played a significant role. When rewards are distributed based on factors other than merit—such as identity, connections, or luck—the motivation to work hard and excel is diminished. This shift away from meritocracy fosters a culture where mediocrity is tolerated and even rewarded, leading to a decline in overall competence across society.

The Importance of Individual Responsibility

Individual responsibility is the foundation upon which competence is built. It is the recognition that one's actions and decisions have consequences, and that success is the result of effort, discipline, and perseverance. When individuals take responsibility for their own lives, they are more likely to develop the skills, knowledge, and attitudes necessary to succeed in a complex and competitive world.

Restoring individual responsibility is essential for reversing the competency crisis because it re-establishes the link between effort and reward. When people understand that their success depends on their own actions, they are more likely to invest in their own development, seek out opportunities for growth, and push themselves to achieve their full potential. This, in turn, leads to higher levels of competence across all sectors of society, from education and industry to government and the arts.

Moreover, individual responsibility fosters a culture of accountability, where people are held to high standards and are expected to meet them. In such a culture, mediocrity is not tolerated, and excellence is rewarded. This creates a virtuous cycle where individuals are continually motivated to improve themselves, leading to greater innovation, productivity, and overall societal progress.

Practical Steps to Restore Individual Responsibility

Restoring individual responsibility requires a multifaceted approach that addresses the cultural, educational, and policy factors that have contributed to its decline. Here are some practical steps that can be taken to reclaim the value of individual responsibility:

Educational Reform: Education plays a critical role in shaping the values and attitudes of the next generation. Schools and universities must prioritize the teaching of responsibility, accountability, and the connection between effort and reward. This can be achieved by reintroducing merit-based assessments, setting high academic standards, and encouraging students to take ownership of their learning. Programs that promote personal development, critical thinking, and problem-solving skills should be emphasized, as these are essential for fostering a sense of responsibility.

Promoting Work Ethic and Self-Reliance: Society must celebrate and promote the values of hard work, self-reliance, and perseverance. Public campaigns, media representation, and community initiatives can all play a role in highlighting the importance of these values. Employers can also contribute by creating work environments that reward effort, innovation, and responsibility, and by providing opportunities for professional development and growth.

Reforming Welfare and Social Policies: While safety nets are necessary, welfare and social policies should be designed to encourage self-sufficiency rather than dependency. This can be achieved by implementing policies that provide temporary support while incentivizing work, education, and skill development. Programs that offer job training, education, and entrepreneurship opportunities can help individuals transition from dependency to self-reliance.

Encouraging Entrepreneurship and Innovation: Entrepreneurship is one of the most direct expressions of individual responsibility, as it requires individuals to take risks, make decisions, and be accountable for the outcomes. Governments and private organizations can promote entrepreneurship by reducing regulatory barriers, providing access to capital, and offering mentorship and support for aspiring entrepreneurs. A culture that celebrates innovation and risk-taking will naturally foster greater responsibility and competence.

Leadership by Example: Leaders in all sectors—government, business, education, and community organizations—must model the values of responsibility and accountability. When leaders demonstrate a commitment to excellence, integrity, and personal responsibility, they set a powerful example for others to follow. Leadership development programs that focus on these values can help cultivate a new generation of responsible leaders.

Strengthening Family and Community Structures: Families and communities play a crucial role in instilling values of responsibility and self-reliance. Strengthening these structures through family support programs, community-building initiatives, and policies that encourage stable family life can help reinforce the importance of individual responsibility from an early age.

The Benefits of Restoring Individual Responsibility

Reclaiming the value of individual responsibility offers numerous benefits for both individuals and society as a whole. For individuals, taking responsibility for one's own life leads to greater self-confidence, resilience, and a sense of purpose. It empowers people to take control of their own destinies, leading to higher levels of personal satisfaction and fulfillment.

For society, a renewed emphasis on individual responsibility leads to higher levels of competence, productivity, and innovation. When people are motivated to improve themselves and take ownership of their actions, they are more likely to contribute positively to their communities and the broader economy. This creates a more dynamic, resilient, and prosperous society, capable of meeting the challenges of the future.

Moreover, restoring individual responsibility can help rebuild social trust and cohesion. When people are held accountable for their actions and are rewarded for their efforts, there is greater respect for the rule of law, social norms, and the principles of fairness and justice. This fosters a sense of shared purpose and mutual respect, which are essential for maintaining a stable and harmonious society.

Reinvigorating Meritocracy: The Necessity of Re-Establishing Merit-Based Systems to Foster Innovation and Excellence

Meritocracy—the principle that individuals should advance based on their abilities, efforts, and achievements—has been a cornerstone of Western progress and prosperity. It is the engine that drives innovation, excellence, and social mobility, ensuring that the most capable and hardworking individuals rise to the top and contribute to the betterment of society. However, in recent decades, the erosion of meritocratic principles across various sectors—education, business, politics, and beyond—has led to a decline in innovation, a stifling of excellence, and an overall competency crisis. To address these challenges and secure a prosperous future, it is imperative to reinvigorate meritocracy across all sectors of society.

The Erosion of Meritocracy

Meritocracy has come under attack from various quarters, leading to its gradual erosion. Several factors have contributed to this decline:

Identity Politics and Affirmative Action: The rise of identity politics has led to a focus on factors such as race, gender, and other identity markers rather than on individual merit. Affirmative action policies, while well-intentioned in their aim to redress historical injustices, have often resulted in the selection of candidates based on identity rather than on merit. This has created a culture where individuals are rewarded not for their abilities or achievements but for their membership in certain groups.

Entitlement Culture: The growing sense of entitlement in Western societies has led to the devaluation of hard work and excellence. When individuals believe they are owed success regardless of their efforts, the motivation to strive for excellence diminishes. This has fostered a culture of mediocrity, where everyone is expected to receive equal rewards, regardless of their contributions.

Bureaucratization and Nepotism: In many organizations, particularly in government and large corporations, meritocracy has been undermined by bureaucratization and nepotism. Hiring, promotions, and rewards are often based on connections, seniority, or adherence to bureaucratic procedures rather than on actual performance or potential. This stifles innovation and discourages talented individuals from pursuing leadership roles.

Educational Policies: The shift in educational priorities from academic rigor to inclusivity and self-esteem has led to the lowering of standards and the de-emphasis of competition. Grade inflation, the elimination of standardized testing, and the avoidance of failure have all contributed to the erosion of meritocracy in education, with long-term consequences for the workforce and society at large.

The Importance of Meritocracy

Meritocracy is essential for fostering innovation and excellence. When individuals are rewarded based on their abilities and efforts, they are motivated to push the boundaries of what is possible, to innovate, and to excel. This drive for excellence is what has propelled Western societies to the forefront of technological, scientific, and cultural advancements.

Meritocracy also ensures that the most capable individuals occupy positions of leadership and influence. In a meritocratic system, leaders are chosen not based on their connections or identity but on their ability to solve problems, inspire others, and achieve results. This leads to more effective governance, better decision-making, and a more dynamic and competitive economy.

Moreover, meritocracy promotes social mobility and fairness. It provides individuals from all backgrounds with the opportunity to rise based on their talents and hard work, rather than on their social status or identity. This fosters a sense of fairness and justice in society, reducing social tensions and promoting social cohesion.

The Necessity of Re-Establishing Merit-Based Systems

To reinvigorate meritocracy, it is necessary to re-establish merit-based systems across all sectors of society. This involves a return to principles that prioritize competence, effort, and achievement over identity, connections, or entitlements. Here are some key areas where meritocracy must be reasserted:

Education: The education system is the foundation of a meritocratic society. To re-establish meritocracy in education, schools and universities must set high academic standards and hold students accountable for their performance. This includes reintroducing rigorous assessments, rewarding academic excellence, and ensuring that grades and honors are awarded based on merit rather than on identity or effort alone. Educational institutions should also promote competition and provide opportunities for students to excel, whether through scholarships, advanced placement programs, or other merit-based initiatives.

Hiring and Promotion Practices: In the workplace, merit-based hiring and promotion practices are essential for ensuring that the most capable individuals rise to positions of leadership. Employers should prioritize skills, experience, and performance in their hiring and promotion decisions, rather than relying on identity, connections, or seniority. This can be achieved through transparent and objective evaluation processes, such as performance reviews, competency-based assessments, and peer evaluations. Additionally, organizations should promote a culture that values innovation, results, and accountability, rewarding employees who demonstrate excellence and contribute to the organization's success.

Government and Public Sector: Meritocracy must be reasserted in government and the public sector to ensure effective governance and public trust. This involves reducing bureaucratic inertia and nepotism by implementing merit-based recruitment and promotion practices. Public servants should be selected and advanced based on their competence, experience, and ability to serve the public good, rather than on political connections or adherence to bureaucratic procedures. Additionally, meritocracy in government can be promoted through accountability measures, such as performance audits, transparency initiatives, and the elimination of corruption and patronage.

Corporate Governance: In the corporate world, meritocracy is essential for driving innovation, competitiveness, and long-term success. Companies should prioritize merit in their governance practices, ensuring that leadership positions are filled by individuals who have demonstrated the ability to achieve results and drive growth. This involves implementing merit-based selection processes for board members, executives, and managers, as well as fostering a corporate culture that rewards innovation, risk-taking, and accountability. Companies should also invest in talent development programs that provide opportunities for employees to advance based on their skills and performance.

Public Policy and Legislation: Public policy should support and promote meritocracy by encouraging competition, innovation, and individual responsibility. This includes reforming policies that undermine meritocracy, such as affirmative action and entitlement programs, and replacing them with initiatives that promote equal opportunity and reward excellence. Governments should also invest in education, research, and infrastructure that support innovation and economic growth, ensuring that individuals and businesses have the resources and incentives to excel.

The Benefits of Reinvigorating Meritocracy

Reinvigorating meritocracy offers numerous benefits for individuals, organizations, and society as a whole. By re-establishing merit-based systems, we can:

Foster Innovation and Creativity: When individuals are rewarded based on their abilities and efforts, they are more likely to take risks, pursue new ideas, and push the boundaries of what is possible. This drive for innovation leads to technological advancements, scientific breakthroughs, and cultural achievements that benefit society as a whole.

Promote Excellence and Accountability: Meritocracy ensures that individuals are held to high standards and are rewarded for their achievements. This promotes a culture of excellence, where individuals are motivated to perform at their best and are accountable for their actions. This leads to more effective organizations, better decision-making, and higher levels of productivity and performance.

Enhance Social Mobility and Fairness: Meritocracy provides individuals from all backgrounds with the opportunity to succeed based on their talents and hard work. This promotes social mobility and reduces inequality, ensuring that success is not determined by social status or identity but by individual merit. This fosters a sense of fairness and justice in society, reducing social tensions and promoting social cohesion.

Strengthen Economic Competitiveness: Meritocracy drives economic growth and competitiveness by ensuring that the most capable individuals occupy positions of leadership and influence. This leads to more innovative and dynamic economies, where businesses are able to compete globally and create jobs and wealth for society.

Restore Public Trust and Confidence: Reinvigorating meritocracy can help restore public trust and confidence in institutions, organizations, and government. When individuals see that success is based on merit rather than on identity, connections, or entitlements, they are more likely to trust and respect the institutions that govern them. This promotes social cohesion, stability, and a sense of shared purpose.

Revitalizing the Entrepreneurial Spirit: Strategies for Reigniting the Force That Once Drove Western Progress and Prosperity

The entrepreneurial spirit—characterized by innovation, risk-taking, and the drive to create and grow new ventures—has been a key driver of Western progress and prosperity. From the industrial revolution to the tech booms of the 20th and 21st centuries, entrepreneurship has fueled economic growth, job creation, and societal advancement. However, in recent decades, this spirit has waned in many parts of the Western world, stifled by a combination of cultural, economic, and regulatory challenges. To restore the dynamism that once propelled the West to global leadership, it is crucial to reignite the entrepreneurial spirit through targeted strategies that address these barriers and foster a culture of innovation and enterprise.

The Decline of the Entrepreneurial Spirit

Several factors have contributed to the decline of entrepreneurship in the West:

Cultural Shifts: The rise of a risk-averse culture, fueled by the expansion of welfare states and a focus on job security, has led to a decline in the willingness to take the risks necessary for entrepreneurial ventures. This cultural shift has been accompanied by an increased emphasis on career stability over innovation, discouraging many from pursuing entrepreneurial paths.

Regulatory Burdens: Overregulation and bureaucratic red tape have made it increasingly difficult for entrepreneurs to start and grow businesses. Complex tax codes, stringent labor laws, and an array of regulations often discourage would-be entrepreneurs from taking the leap, as the costs and risks associated with compliance can be prohibitive.

Access to Capital: Despite the proliferation of venture capital and startup funding in certain sectors, access to capital remains a significant barrier for many entrepreneurs, particularly those outside major tech hubs. Traditional financial institutions have become more risk-averse since the global financial crisis, making it harder for small and medium-sized enterprises (SMEs) to secure the funding they need to innovate and expand.

Educational Gaps: The education system in many Western countries has traditionally emphasized academic achievement over entrepreneurial skills. While there has been some progress in incorporating entrepreneurship into curricula, many students still graduate without the practical skills, financial literacy, or mindset needed to succeed as entrepreneurs.

Global Competition: The rise of emerging markets, particularly in Asia, has shifted the global economic landscape. These regions have embraced entrepreneurship with vigor, creating competitive pressures that have further challenged Western entrepreneurs. The rapid pace of technological change has also made it more difficult for new businesses to gain a foothold, as they must compete with established players with significant resources and global reach.

Strategies for Reigniting the Entrepreneurial Spirit

To revitalize the entrepreneurial spirit in the West, a comprehensive approach is needed that addresses cultural, regulatory, financial, and educational barriers. Here are key strategies that can help reignite the drive to innovate and create:

Promoting a Culture of Entrepreneurship:

Public Awareness Campaigns: Governments, educational institutions, and private organizations can collaborate on campaigns that celebrate entrepreneurship and highlight its importance to economic growth and innovation. By showcasing success stories, emphasizing the value of risk-taking, and demystifying the entrepreneurial process, these campaigns can inspire a new generation to pursue entrepreneurial ventures.

Mentorship and Role Models: Successful entrepreneurs can play a crucial role in mentoring aspiring business owners and serving as role models. Creating networks and programs that connect experienced entrepreneurs with newcomers can help transfer knowledge, provide support, and reduce the fear of failure.

Regulatory and Tax Reforms:

Simplifying Regulations: Streamlining the regulatory environment is essential to making entrepreneurship more accessible. Governments should review existing regulations to eliminate unnecessary barriers, reduce compliance costs, and simplify processes for starting and running businesses. One-stop shops for business registration, licensing, and compliance can make it easier for entrepreneurs to navigate regulatory requirements.

Tax Incentives for Startups: Tax policies can be designed to encourage entrepreneurship by offering incentives such as tax breaks, credits, and deductions for startups and small businesses. Reducing the tax burden on new businesses during their critical early years can help them grow and reinvest in innovation.

Improving Access to Capital:

Expanding Funding Opportunities: Governments and financial institutions can work together to expand access to capital for entrepreneurs. This includes promoting alternative financing options such as crowdfunding, peer-to-peer lending, and microloans. Public-private partnerships can also help create funding pools specifically targeted at startups and SMEs in underserved sectors or regions.

Supporting Venture Capital and Angel Investment: Encouraging the growth of venture capital and angel investment ecosystems is crucial for funding high-growth startups. Governments can incentivize investment in startups through tax breaks, matching funds, or co-investment schemes, particularly in regions where venture capital is scarce.

Enhancing Entrepreneurial Education:

Integrating Entrepreneurship into Education: Schools and universities should incorporate entrepreneurship education into their curricula, teaching students the skills needed to start and manage businesses. This includes practical skills such as financial literacy, business planning, marketing, and negotiation, as well as fostering a mindset that embraces creativity, problem-solving, and resilience.

Experiential Learning Opportunities: Educational institutions can offer experiential learning opportunities such as business incubators, startup competitions, and internships with startups. These programs allow students to gain hands-on experience in the entrepreneurial world, building confidence and practical skills.

Fostering Innovation Ecosystems:

Creating Innovation Hubs: Governments and private sector partners can establish innovation hubs or clusters that bring together entrepreneurs, investors, researchers, and industry leaders. These hubs can provide the infrastructure, resources, and networks needed to support innovation and collaboration. Examples include Silicon Valley in the United States and the Tech City in London, which have become global centers of entrepreneurship.

Encouraging Research and Development (R&D): R&D is critical to innovation and the creation of new businesses. Governments can incentivize R&D through grants, tax credits, and subsidies, particularly for startups and SMEs. Collaboration between universities, research institutions, and industry can also help bridge the gap between research and commercialization.

Reducing Barriers to Global Markets:

Promoting Trade and Export Opportunities: Expanding access to global markets is essential for entrepreneurs looking to scale their businesses. Governments can support startups by providing export assistance, reducing trade barriers, and negotiating favorable trade agreements. Additionally, programs that help startups navigate foreign markets, such as export readiness training and market research support, can facilitate international expansion.

Leveraging Digital Platforms: Digital platforms and e-commerce can help entrepreneurs reach global audiences with minimal overhead. Governments and industry partners can provide training and resources to help startups leverage these platforms effectively, including guidance on digital marketing, logistics, and cross-border trade.

The Benefits of Revitalizing the Entrepreneurial Spirit

Revitalizing the entrepreneurial spirit offers numerous benefits for individuals, economies, and societies:

Economic Growth and Job Creation: Entrepreneurs are key drivers of economic growth and job creation. By fostering new businesses, societies can create jobs, stimulate demand, and drive economic expansion.

Startups and SMEs are particularly important for creating employment opportunities and fostering economic dynamism.

Innovation and Competitiveness: Entrepreneurs bring new ideas, products, and services to market, driving innovation and competitiveness. By encouraging entrepreneurship, societies can remain at the forefront of technological and industrial advancements, ensuring long-term prosperity and global leadership.

Social Mobility and Inclusivity: Entrepreneurship provides a pathway for individuals from diverse backgrounds to achieve economic independence and success. By lowering barriers to entry and providing support for underrepresented groups, societies can promote social mobility and inclusivity, reducing inequality and fostering a more equitable economy.

Resilience and Adaptability: A strong entrepreneurial ecosystem enhances a society's resilience and adaptability to change. Entrepreneurs are often at the forefront of responding to economic shifts, technological disruptions, and societal challenges, providing innovative solutions that help societies navigate uncertainty and thrive in the face of adversity.

11

The Fork in the Road

The West at a Critical Juncture Between Decline and a Return to Greatness

Once the undisputed leader in economic power, cultural influence, and technological innovation, we now stand at a critical juncture. Decades of cultural shifts, economic challenges, and geopolitical pressures have brought the West to a point where it must make a fundamental choice: continue down a path of decline, marked by the erosion of the values that once drove its success, or return to those foundational principles and reclaim its position as a global leader. The decisions made in the coming years will determine whether the West remains a beacon of progress and prosperity or fades into irrelevance.

The Path of Decline

The signs of decline are already evident across much of the Western world. Economic stagnation, social fragmentation, political instability, and a loss of confidence in the future all point to a civilization that has lost its way. Several factors have contributed to this decline:

Cultural Erosion: The erosion of the values that once defined Western civilization—such as individual responsibility, meritocracy, and the pursuit of excellence—has led to a culture where mediocrity is tolerated and even celebrated. The rise of entitlement, victimhood, and identity politics has undermined the social cohesion and shared purpose that are essential for a thriving society.

Economic Stagnation: Many Western economies have struggled with slow growth, high debt levels, and declining productivity. The overregulation of markets, the expansion of welfare states, and the devaluation of work and entrepreneurship have stifled innovation and economic dynamism. This has led to rising inequality, joblessness, and a sense of economic insecurity among large segments of the population.

Political Instability: Political polarization and the erosion of trust in institutions have created an environment where governance is increasingly dysfunctional. The inability of governments to address pressing issues—such as immigration, economic reform, and social inequality—has fueled populism and extremism, further destabilizing Western democracies.

Geopolitical Weakness: The West's geopolitical influence has waned as emerging powers, particularly in Asia, have risen. The failure to maintain a strong and coherent foreign policy, coupled with military overreach and strategic blunders, has weakened the West's position on the global stage. This has emboldened adversaries and created a more volatile international environment.

Technological Disruption: While the West remains a leader in technological innovation, the rapid pace of technological change has also created challenges. Automation, artificial intelligence, and the gig economy have disrupted traditional industries and labor markets, leading to job displacement and social unrest. The failure to adapt to these changes and to ensure that the benefits of technology are widely shared has contributed to social and economic instability.

The Path to Renewal

Despite these challenges, the West has the potential to reverse its decline and return to greatness. This requires a return to the values and principles that once made it the most dynamic and prosperous civilization in history. The path to renewal involves several key strategies:

Reasserting Core Values: The West must reaffirm the values that have historically driven its success—individual responsibility, meritocracy, the pursuit of excellence, and the rule of law. This requires a cultural shift away from entitlement and victimhood, and toward a renewed emphasis on hard work, personal accountability, and the rewards of merit. By celebrating and rewarding those who contribute to society through innovation, creativity, and perseverance, the West can rebuild a culture of excellence.

Economic Reform and Innovation: Economic renewal is essential for reversing the West's decline. This involves reducing regulatory burdens, encouraging entrepreneurship, and promoting innovation. Governments must create an environment where businesses can thrive, where new industries can emerge, and where individuals are incentivized to take risks and create value. This includes tax reforms, investments in education and infrastructure, and policies that promote competition and free markets.

Strengthening Social Cohesion: The West must address the social fragmentation that has contributed to its decline. This involves fostering a sense of shared purpose and national identity, as well as addressing the root causes of social inequality. Policies that promote social mobility, education, and community engagement can help bridge the divides that have emerged in Western societies. By focusing on what unites rather than what divides, the West can rebuild the social fabric that is essential for a stable and prosperous society.

Restoring Political Integrity: Political renewal is critical for the West's future. This requires restoring trust in institutions, reducing corruption, and promoting transparency and accountability in government. Political leaders must prioritize the common good over partisan interests, and work to address the real concerns of their citizens. This includes reforming electoral systems, reducing the influence of money in politics, and promoting civic engagement.

Reasserting Global Leadership: The West must reclaim its position as a global leader by adopting a coherent and strategic foreign policy. This involves strengthening alliances, promoting democratic values, and engaging in responsible global governance. The West must also invest in its military and diplomatic capabilities to deter adversaries and promote stability in key regions. By leading on issues such as climate change, human rights, and technological innovation, the West can regain its moral authority and influence on the global stage.

Adapting to Technological Change: The West must embrace technological innovation while ensuring that its benefits are widely shared. This involves investing in education and training programs that equip workers with the skills needed for the jobs of the future. Governments must also promote policies that encourage responsible innovation and address the ethical and social implications of new technologies. By harnessing the power of technology, the West can drive economic growth, improve quality of life, and solve some of the most pressing challenges facing humanity.

The Stakes of the Choice

The stakes of the choice before the West could not be higher. The path of decline leads to a future of diminished influence, economic stagnation, social unrest, and geopolitical instability. If the West continues on its current trajectory, it risks losing its position as a global leader, with far-reaching consequences for the international order and the values of democracy, freedom, and human rights that it has long championed.

On the other hand, the path to renewal offers the opportunity to reclaim the West's greatness. By returning to its core values, embracing innovation, and addressing the challenges of the 21st century, the West can once again become a beacon of progress and prosperity. This path requires difficult choices, bold leadership, and a willingness to confront the forces of mediocrity and decline. But the rewards of this path are immense—a stronger, more dynamic, and more just society, capable of leading the world in the decades to come.

Reject the Looter Mentality, Embrace Competence, and Take Responsibility for the Future of Western Civilization

Western civilization stands at a crossroads, facing a critical choice that will determine its future. The path of decline, marked by the rise of a looter mentality—a mindset that seeks to take without earning, to demand without contributing—leads to mediocrity, stagnation, and the erosion of everything that once made the West great. In contrast, the path of renewal, rooted in the values of competence, responsibility, and individual achievement, offers the promise of a vibrant, prosperous, and resilient civilization. The time has come to make a decisive choice: to reject the looter mentality and embrace the principles that have driven Western success for centuries.

Rejecting the Looter Mentality

The looter mentality has taken hold in many corners of Western society, manifesting in entitlement, victimhood, and a culture that rewards mediocrity over merit. This mindset is antithetical to the values of hard work, innovation, and excellence that have historically propelled the West to greatness. The looter mentality encourages individuals to seek benefits without effort, to demand rewards without merit, and to blame others for their own shortcomings. It is a mindset that erodes the very foundations of a prosperous society, leading to economic stagnation, social fragmentation, and a loss of personal agency.

Rejecting the looter mentality requires a cultural shift—one that recognizes the inherent dignity and value of work, the importance of personal responsibility, and the necessity of earning one's place in society. It means rejecting the notion that success is a matter of luck or privilege, and instead embracing the idea that success is earned through effort, determination, and the pursuit of excellence. It means holding oneself and others accountable, and demanding that rewards and recognition be based on merit, not entitlement.

Embracing Competence

Competence is the cornerstone of a thriving society. It is the ability to do something well, to achieve results, and to contribute meaningfully to the world around us. Competence is not a matter of chance; it is the product of education, training, experience, and a relentless commitment to self-improvement. In a world that often prioritizes appearances, connections, or identity over actual ability, it is more important than ever to reaffirm the value of competence.

Embracing competence means prioritizing meritocracy in all aspects of society. It means ensuring that positions of leadership, influence, and responsibility are filled by those who have demonstrated the ability to excel. It means creating environments—whether in schools, workplaces, or communities—where excellence is rewarded, and where individuals are encouraged to strive for greatness. Competence must become the standard by which success is measured, and mediocrity must no longer be tolerated.

Taking Responsibility for the Future

The future of Western civilization depends on the choices we make today. Taking responsibility means recognizing that we each have a role to play in shaping that future. It means understanding that the decisions we make—how we work, how we raise our children, how we engage with our communities—will determine the course of our society for generations to come.

Taking responsibility requires a commitment to the principles that have made the West successful: individual liberty, personal accountability, and the pursuit of excellence. It means rejecting the easy path of blame and entitlement and instead embracing the challenges of self-reliance, hard work, and innovation. It means teaching these values to the next generation, ensuring that they understand the importance of earning their place in the world and contributing to the greater good.

But taking responsibility also means recognizing that we are not alone in this effort. The strength of Western civilization has always come from the collective contributions of individuals who, together, build strong communities, innovative economies, and resilient societies. By working together, by supporting each other in our efforts to excel, we can create a future that honors the achievements of the past while forging new paths to progress and prosperity.

The Urgency of the Moment

The choices before us are stark, and the stakes could not be higher. The decline of Western civilization is not inevitable; it is the result of choices—choices to prioritize short-term gains over long-term stability, to reward mediocrity over excellence, to accept the status quo rather than challenge it. But just as decline is the result of choices, so too is renewal.

The time for action is now. We cannot afford to delay, to wait for others to solve the problems we face. Each of us has the power to make a difference, to reject the looter mentality, to embrace competence, and to take responsibility for the future. By doing so, we can ensure that the West remains a beacon of progress, a model of prosperity, and a defender of the values that have made it great.

A Call to Action

To all who read these words: this is your call to action. The future of Western civilization depends on your choices, your actions, your commitment to the values that have driven progress for centuries. Reject the looter mentality that saps our strength and undermines our potential. Embrace competence, strive for excellence, and take responsibility for your life and the world around you.

The road to renewal is not easy, but it is the only path to a future of prosperity, innovation, and greatness. The time to act is now, and the choice is yours. Will you stand up for the principles that have made the West the most dynamic and successful civilization in history? Will you take responsibility for ensuring that those principles continue to guide us into the future?

If the answer is yes, then the work begins today. Together, we can restore the values of individual responsibility, meritocracy, and excellence. Together, we can rebuild a society that rewards hard work, celebrates achievement, and fosters innovation. Together, we can ensure that the West not only survives but thrives in the years to come.

The future is in our hands. Let us seize it with the determination, the competence, and the responsibility that have always defined the best of Western civilization.

As the West stands at a pivotal juncture, grappling with the forces of decline and the challenges of renewal, Ayn Rand's philosophy emerges as a powerful guiding light for those who seek to restore Western civilization to its rightful place as a leader in the world. Rand's ideas, rooted in the principles of individualism, rational self-interest, and the pursuit of excellence, offer a clear and compelling framework for addressing the cultural, economic, and political crises that threaten the West today.

The Power of Individualism

At the heart of Ayn Rand's philosophy is the belief in the sanctity and power of the individual. Rand championed the idea that each person is an end in themselves, with the right to live their life according to their own values, free from coercion or oppression. This belief in individualism is the foundation of a free and prosperous society, where individuals are empowered to pursue their own happiness, to innovate, and to achieve greatness.

In a world increasingly dominated by collectivist ideologies and identity politics, Rand's emphasis on the individual is more relevant than ever. The West's success has always been driven by the creativity, ambition, and determination of individuals who refused to be bound by the constraints of conformity or mediocrity. By reaffirming the importance of individualism, we can restore the spirit of innovation and excellence that has defined Western civilization for centuries.

Rational Self-Interest as a Moral Imperative

Rand's philosophy also challenges the conventional moral code that often condemns self-interest as selfish or immoral. Instead, Rand argued that rational self-interest—pursuing one's own happiness and well-being through productive and ethical means—is not only moral but essential for a thriving society. When individuals are free to pursue their own interests, they create value, drive progress, and contribute to the prosperity of society as a whole.

This concept of rational self-interest is a powerful antidote to the looter mentality that has taken hold in many parts of the West. By rejecting the idea that individuals are entitled to the fruits of others' labor and instead embracing the principle that success must be earned, we can foster a culture of personal responsibility and achievement. In doing so, we can create a society where individuals are motivated to excel, to innovate, and to contribute to the common good.

The Pursuit of Excellence

Excellence, for Rand, was not a luxury but a necessity. She believed that human beings have the capacity for greatness, and that the pursuit of excellence in all areas of life—work, art, science, and relationships—is the highest moral purpose. Rand's heroes, such as John Galt and Howard Roark, embody this relentless pursuit of excellence, refusing to compromise their vision or values in the face of mediocrity or opposition.

In a world that often rewards conformity and mediocrity, Rand's celebration of excellence serves as a rallying cry for those who seek to restore the West to its former glory. By demanding the best from ourselves and others, by refusing to settle for anything less than greatness, we can reignite the entrepreneurial spirit, the intellectual rigor, and the creative genius that have made the West the most dynamic and prosperous civilization in history.

The Role of Reason and Objective Reality

Central to Rand's philosophy is the role of reason and objective reality as the basis for knowledge, ethics, and action. Rand rejected mysticism, relativism, and any form of irrationality, arguing that reason is humanity's most powerful tool for understanding the world and achieving success. In a time when truth is often distorted by ideology, propaganda, and emotion, Rand's unwavering commitment to reason is a beacon for those who seek to navigate the complexities of the modern world.

By embracing reason and objective reality, we can cut through the confusion and chaos that often characterize contemporary discourse. We can make decisions based on facts, evidence, and logic, rather than on the whims of popular opinion or the demands of interest groups. This rational approach is essential for effective governance, sound economic policy, and the pursuit of justice.

A Call to Action

Ayn Rand's philosophy offers a powerful framework for those who are committed to restoring the West to its rightful place as a leader in the world. By embracing individualism, rational self-interest, the pursuit of excellence, and the power of reason, we can build a society that rewards competence, innovation, and achievement.

The challenges we face are significant, but so too are the opportunities. The West has the potential to reclaim its greatness, to lead the world in innovation, prosperity, and freedom. But this will require a return to the values and principles that have historically driven Western success—a return to the philosophy that Ayn Rand so passionately advocated.

As we stand at this critical fork in the road, let us be guided by the light of Rand's philosophy. Let us reject the forces of mediocrity, entitlement, and decline, and instead embrace the path of individual responsibility, competence, and excellence. The future of Western civilization depends on it.

In the words of Rand herself: "The question isn't who is going to let me; it's who is going to stop me." Let us take this as our rallying cry as we work to restore the West to its rightful place as a beacon of progress, innovation, and freedom. The time to act is now, and the choice is ours.

www.ingramcontent.com/pod-product-compliance
Lightning Source LLC
Chambersburg PA
CBHW060938120626
46557CB00003B/1053